# An Outline of 2000 Years of Turkish History

D1108750

by

Süleyman Seydi

REPUBLIC OF TURKEY
MINISTRY OF CULTURE AND TOURISM PUBLICATIONS

© Republic of Turkey Ministry of Culture and Tourism
General Directorate of Libraries and Publications
3098


Handbook Series
1

ISBN 978-975-17-3274-3

www.kulturturizm.gov.tr
E-mail: yayimlar@kulturturizm.gov.tr

---

Seydi, Süleyman
An outline of 2000 years of Turkish
history / Süleyman Seydi.- Ankara:
Ministry of Culture and Tourism, 2008.

168 p.; 20 cm.- (Ministry of Culture
and Tourism Publications; 3098.
Directorate General of Libraries and
Publications handbook series; 1)
ISBN 978-975-17-3274-3
I. Title. II. Series.
956.1

---

Cover Picture:
The Museum of Topkapi Palace Collection
Istanbul / Turkey

Printed by: Remark Reklamcılık Prodüksiyon
Yayıncılık Ticaret LTD. ŞTİ.

Second Edition
Print run: 5000

Printed in *Ankara* in 2008

# Table of Contents

## Note on Usage

Modern Turkish use the Latin alphabet, modified to ensure that there is a separate letter for each main sound. The spelling thus aims at phonetic consistency. Consonants have no more or less the same sound as in English, except that:

c   *like j in English*
ç   *like ch in English*
ğ   *the "soft g". depending on the adjoining letters, this is dropped, pronounced like y in English, or treated a lengthening the preceding vowel.*
ı   *is a back, close, unrounded vowel which does not exist in English, the nearest equivalent being the phantom vowel in the second syllable of rhythm (in Turkish translation ritim)*
ö   *like ö in German or eu in French peur*
ş   *like sh in English*
ü   *like ü in German or u in French*

# Introduction

Turks have played crucial roles in history. Throughout the thousands of years of their history, Turks have founded more than a hundred small and large states on the continents of Asia, Europe and Africa. One of the prominent states that was established by the Turks in the early period of their history was the Greater Hun Empire. The Greater Seljuk Empire and the Ottoman Empire were other preeminent Turkish states that were founded during the Islamic period. The Ottoman Empire succeeded in creating a peaceful atmosphere over three continents, stretching over 20 million square kilometers, for nearly four centuries with people from different religious and ethnic origins. These features of the Ottoman state put it among the greatest and most powerful political formations that have ever been recorded in history, comparable only to the Roman and British Empires. Although it was the only remarkable Islamic state in the world at the beginning of twentieth century, the Ottoman Turks remained behind the contemporary modern world that arose in the West. This was also valid for the Turkish world that was outside of the Ottoman Empire's boundaries.

Ottoman statesmen and intellectuals began a modernization process in the eighteenth century in order to escape from awkward positions. Modernization was paralleled by the raising values of secularism, laicism and nationalism, which all became fundamental to the shaping of the modern Turkish world. The First World War was one of the biggest turning points in all of Turkish history since the Turks lost their largest state. Following the war, their homeland in the Anatolian peninsula was occupied by western-backed Greek troops. However, under the charismatic leadership of Mustafa Kemal Atatürk, Anatolian Turks struggled for their an independent of homeland based on the regions of Anatolia in which they had lived for nearly a thousand year, and founded the Turkish Republic as a nation state. Following a series of reform processes, Turkey has been on the verge of accession to the European Union as one of the only democratic, secular state in the Islamic world.

The concept of "Turks" does not only refer to the people who live in the modern Turkish Republic, but also to those people with some tie to Turkish culture who live outside Turkey's borders in either independent states or as subjects of other nations. World history shows us that the peoples who have spoken some variant of the Turkish language can be found under many different names, including the Huns, the Tabgachs, the Uyghurs, the Karahans, the Seljuks, the Ottomans, the Tatars, the Kyrgyz, the Uzbek, the Turkmen, the Yakuts, the Chuvash and the Pomaks. The Turks in their history have never been united under one flag or contained within a single political boundary. This has been the case ever since the time of the Turkish peoples' ancient history in the Asian steppes, as well for the periods of the Hun, Göktürk, Seljuk and Ottoman empires. The same still holds true today if we consider the Turkish nation-state and the number of Turks living outside its borders.

It is widely believed that the term "Turks" refers to a political entity rather than to an ethnic identity. After the founding of the Göktürk state, the term "Turks" was first used as the name of that state, then for those Turkish nomadic societies who had been the subjects of the Göktürks with their own names. In the course of time, the term "Turks" became a name that was applicable to all societies tied to Turkish groups. Today there persists a common distinction between the terms "Turks" (Turkish) and "Turki" (Turkic). "Turks" refers only to those Turkish people living within the modern Turkish Republic. "Turki" refers to all Turkish people in the world - both inside and outside the Turkish Republic. The division of the larger Turkish people into two groups - according to whether or not they live within the Turkish Republic - is inherited from 19th century Russian imperialists, who had their own political motives for differentiating the Turks of Russia from those of the Ottoman Empire. These divisive terms continued to be used throughout the Soviet period in Russian history, and have become even more apparent in the politics of the post-Soviet Russian Federation. One may claim that this kind of distinction may be unavoidable in order to distinguish between the Turks of Turkey and all Turks everywhere. This does not however, change the fact that the term "Turks" (Turkish) is applicable to all Turkish people wherever they live. Today's Turkish worlds occupy a broad belt of territories extending across Asia from the eastern Mediterranean to Mongolia and reaching northward to the Middle Volga basin and the Siberian borderline of Kazakhstan. Within these areas there are six independent Turkish states apart from the modern Turkish Republic, these include Azerbaijan, Kazakhstan, Kyrgyzstan, Turkmenistan, Uzbekistan, and the Turkish Republic of Northern Cyprus (which is only recognized by the

Republic of Turkey). There are several Turkish autonomous republics, these include Bashkir, Chuvash, Yakut, Tatar, Kabardino-Balkaria, Kara-Kalpak, Nakhichevan, Tuva and

Xingjian Uigur. There are several Turkish autonomous regions, these include the Altai Republic, Karachay-Cherkessia, Khahass, Gagauz and Nogorno-Karabakh in Azerbaijan which came under Armenian occupation in 1991. Some other Turkish people are the Crimean Tatars, the Karaim and the Krymchaks in the Crimean Peninsula, the Meshetian Turks, the Nogai and the Kumky in the Dagestan Autonomous Republic. In addition, there are several Turkish-inhabited regions in Iran, Iraq, Georgia, Bulgaria, Greece, Macedonia, Tajikistan, Afghanistan, and Western Mongolia.

## The Origins of the Turks

The origin and identity of the contemporary Turkish Republic has a history that goes back to the earliest Turks and their precursors in Inner Asia. The exact location of the original motherland of the Turks before their westward migrations is a matter of discussion among scholars from different disciplines. By taking Chinese records into account, historians have established the Altai Mountains and its environs as the boundary of the Turkish motherland. Soviet archeologists shed some light on where the Turkish Motherland was as well. According to them, the prototype of Turkish culture could be found in the Andronovo culture in the Munisinks region in the northwestern Altai Mountains in 1700 -1200 BC. The Andronovo culture emerged from an earlier Afanasyevo culture dating from 2500 - 1700 BC. The Afanasyevo culture was composed of a belligerent-brachycephalic white race with distinct characteristics from the dolichocephalic races of Mongolia and the Mediterranean. The descendents of the brachycephalic race live in the southwestern Altai Mountains.

The earliest date of Turkish history, unfortunately, has not been well documented. However, the first known Turkish people, namely the Saka (Scythians), were living in the vicinity of Khazar and in different regions of Inner Asia in the eighth century B.C. The name Hsiung-nu (Xiongnu) appears in early Chinese sources (2000 B.C.) and was applied to the people living in the western and northwestern parts of China. Although there is debate among scholars on whether the origins of the Hsiung-nu were Mongolian or Turkish it is unanimously accepted that the term described a mixture of Turks and Mongols plus nomadic peoples of related stock. It is believed that the founding and ruling component of the Hsiung-nu were Turks.

Beginning in Inner Asia, the Turks were forced to migrate from their motherland to different places, mostly directed towards the West, and this migration continued over the centuries. A shortage of available lands, scarcity in the face of rising populations, and the need to move about with their grazing animals could couple with wars, either with foreign forces or amongst themselves to bring about the migrations of nomadic and semi-nomadic Turkish tribes. These migrations may be divided into two parts, as those which were carried out in ancient times (pre-0 B.C.) and after (post-0 C.).

According to archeological findings, the first great migration of the Turks reached the western portion of present-day China and Turkistan in the early 2000s B.C. Prior to this migration the Turks had already established themselves in the Altai Mountains, in the Tien Shan Mountains (Celestial in English, Tangri Tagh in the Uyghur language), in Kazakhstan and in Harezm (south of Khwarezm). Another mass migration to the west began in the following centuries after the collapse of the first Turkish empire of Central Asia: the Asian Hun Empire.

If we look at the historical trajectory of the Turkish people from the vantage point of historical starting points, we see not one route ending in the West but several radiating routes beginning in eastern Inner Asia, interconnecting along the way, and ending at points all across Eurasia and around the world.

Some Turkish tribes migrated to Eastern Europe and the Balkans via the lands north of the Black Sea, where they founded powerful states such as the Western Hun Empire, the

Avars' state, and Bulgaria. These Turkish states put pressure on the Western and Eastern portions of the Roman Empire. Other Turkish tribes, such as the Pechenegs and the Kypchaks, stopped and settled in the lands north of the Black Sea areas on their way to the West. Another branch of Turkish tribes, the Ghaznavids, headed towards southwestern Asia. Several Turkish tribes remained in Central Asia. Others, particularly the Oghuz, expanded into Anatolia and founded great states, namely the Seljuk and Ottoman states, which had significant roles in world history.

This book aims to provide an introduction to the whole of Turkish political history by exploring some of its most significant aspects from the earliest times up to the present day. Since the work is aimed at a casual reader, footnotes or endnotes were not used in the text itself, but a bibliography and further reading lists can be found at the end of the book.

# CHAPTER 1

## Ancient Asian Turkish States

### 1. The Hun Empire

In spite of the fact that the first historically recorded Turkish state is that of the Asian Huns in the third century B.C., it is highly probable that many centuries earlier some Turkish people migrated from the Altai area: first to the east, then to the south and the west. These earlier migrations were due to several motives. The Sakas (Scythians), who consisted mainly of Turkish tribes, settled in the area between the Dnieper River and Diniester in the sixth and fourth centuries B.C. The second and most well-known early Turkish state is the Hsiung-nu.

The Hsiung-nu is particularly important because they created the first empire in the Steppes. Turkish scholars unanimously accepted that this was the first organized state that was established by Turks in Central Asia. The Hsiung-nu are referred to as "Hun" by historians after their unification with the Huns in the second half of the fourth century B.C. The first documentation of their history dates from 318 B.C. with the finding of a Chinese account of their agreement with Huns. The first known ruler of the Huns was Tuman (Teoman). His successor was Mete Khan (Mao-tun) (209-174 B.C) under whose leadership the Huns developed an exceptional military.

Mete Khan, the most successful and charismatic leader of the Huns, embarked on a series of conquests. The Huns soon reached the peak of their power and size under Mete Khan's reign. They subjugated Tibet, the Tunghuzs, the Yuechis, and some other tribes. Then Mete Khan turned to China to confront it as an enemy nation. China had previously been able to cope with the Steppes tribes' attack on their territory without great difficulty. However, it could not defend its borders effectively following the unification of the Huns under the leadership of Mete Khan. Having defeated the Chinese army, Mete signed a profitable agreement with China in which the Huns gained control of a significant portion of Chinese territory. China also had to pay tribute to the Huns. In the following years the Huns maintained a constant pressure on the Chinese Empire. During the long-term wars against the Huns, successive Chinese dynasties built several walls, which together constitute the Great Wall of China: a 1,845 kilometer-long military fortification intended to protect China's northern borders against the Huns. Alternately, when the Chinese Empire re-gained its hold on power, the Great Wall also served as a launching pad for aggressive Chinese expansionism northwards.

When Mete Khan died in 174 B.C. the Hun Empire was at its peak of power. The Huns had subordinated twenty six tribes to their authority, including the Chinese, the Mongols and the Tunghuzs over a vast area that extended from Manchuria to the Aral Lake, and from western Siberia to the Gobi Desert. Kiok, Mete's son, tried to strengthen the Hun Empire's power during his reign (174-160 B.C.). First, he exiled the Yuechis from their homeland, and then he invaded China and destroyed the Chinese imperial palace near Chang-an by setting it on fire. During this campaign Kiok married a Chinese princess in order to improve commercial relationships with China. Turkish sources state that this was a political marriage with important consequences for the Huns. As a consequence of this marriage Chinese diplomats and officials gained the right to move freely in the Hun-controlled imperial palace and in Hun-controlled territory. These Chinese diplomats created discord inside the Hun dynasty and among the vassal tribes by engaging in anti-Hun propaganda. Yet the adverse effects of marriage with the Chinese princess would not become apparent in Kiok's own time, but in that of his son Kun-chin (160-126 B.C.). During Kun-chin's reign the Chinese Han Dynasty consolidated its political power and strengthened its military by following the model of the Hun army that had been observed by the Chinese spies inside the Hun Palace: the Han Dynasty began a rigorous program of horse breeding and the formation of a regular cavalry in imitation of the Huns.

One of China's main objectives was to find a new market in the West for its precious silk. To do so it had to secure safe passage on the Silk Road that led to the Mediterranean Sea by way of Inner Asia and Persia. When looked at from this angle, one could not fail to observe that the conflict between the Huns and China was primarily motivated by a struggle for dominance over the lucrative Silk Road. After 120 B.C. the Chinese succeeded in halting the Huns' raids from the north, while also capturing territories along the Silk Road in Inner Asia. The Chinese also stopped paying tribute to the Huns. Eventually the Chinese expanded their goal from defeating the Huns to destroying them. By 110 B.C., the Huns had been forced beyond the Gobi Desert into the northern steppes and forest zones. Things were not the same anymore for the Huns. The Hun Empire's revenues were cut off with the end of tributes from China and by the loss of their most fertile regions to the enemy.

In 60 B.C. a series of pivotal wars began. Now the Chinese demanded recognition of Chinese suzerainty as the condition for further treaties. Chinese pressure and precious gifts to members of the Hun Dynasty created a chaotic environment within the Huns' ruling circles, which led to a partition of the Empire between Ho-han-yeh (58-31) and his older brother Chi-Chi. Ho-Han-yeh's offer for accepting Chinese suzerainty in order to overcome a financial impasse was rejected by the State Council. But at Ho-Han-yeh's insistence, Chi-chi left the country with his people and began to venture towards the West. He established an independent state, called the state of the Western Huns, in the Plain of the Shu-Talas Rivers in 41 B.C. with a new capital which was surrounded by walls. This new state intended to re-create the larger Hun Empire. The newly established state however, was quickly demolished in 36 B.C. by seventy thousand Chinese troops supported by Ho-Han-yeh's men. Some tribes of the Western Huns were forced to migrate to the area between the Aral Lake and the Caspian Sea.

As for Ho-han-yeh's state in the north, it regained its independence from China by expanding to the area between Manchuria to Kashgar during the time of Yu (18 B.C. - 46 A.D). The Huns divided their empire into a northern and a southern state in 48 A.D. Neither state succeeded in centrally unifying itself in the face of increasing Chinese expansion. Soon after, the northern Hun tribes were forced to migrate towards the Aral and Khazar plains. The southern Huns also could not resist China, whose army ended Hun sovereignty in 216. Afterwards, the Huns established a series of short-lived small principalities, such as Hsia, Liang, and Chao until the establishment of the Tabgach (Tabgaç) Turkish state in 315.

After founding their state with Tai as its capital at Shansi, the Tabgach expanded rapidly during the fourth and fifth centuries. Firstly they defeated the remnants of the Hun Empire, then they expanded their sovereignty over Chinese land. The Tabgach invaded Inner Mongolia after defeating Juan-Juan (Ruanruan) in 425, another successor Turkish state of the Huns and later called Avars. Then they conquered the Silk Road by capturing Kansu in 439. The flourishing of Buddhism among the Tabgach people adversely affected their state, as the peaceful nature of Buddhism tended to diminish their military capabilities. The Tabgach state eventually disappeared by the middle of the sixth century under Chinese domination.

One of the Hunnic states was the Akhuns –"White Huns"- (Hephthalites) or the Middle Eastern Huns, founded by the Hunnic people who headed south of the Caspian Sea from the Volga River as the mass of Hunnic people moved to the West. They expanded their boundaries from the Caspian Sea to northern India, Afghanistan, and Inner Asia by the middle of the sixth century. The Akhuns could not defend their territory however, when faced with the Sassanids-Göktürks alliance in 557.

## 2. The Göktürks

The Göktürks, or Kök-Türks, originated from the Ashina tribe, an Altaic people, who lived in the northern corner of the area presently called the Xinjiang Uyghur Autonomous Region of China. The Göktürks were the Huns' descendents, according to Chinese records, and they inherited the Huns' traditions and administrative practices.

The Göktürk state was the first state to bear the name "Turk". This name was to be taken up by many peoples and states later in history. The Göktürk state constituted the second Turkish Empire (the first Turkish Empire being the Hun Empire). The Göktürk state unified all of the Turkish-origin tribes under its administration, except for the Yakut Turks in Eastern Siberia and the Ogur Turks in the West.

The Turks of Central Asia, Turkistan, Transoxiana (Maveraunnehir), northern India, Iran, Anatolia, Iraq, Suriye, and the Balkans were turkified via the Göktürks. "Gök-Türks" is said to mean "Celestial Turks", but this is contested. Alternate meanings are "Blue Turks", or "Numerous Turks" - as "Gök" or "kök" meant both "sky" and "blue" in the Göktürk language.

The first Göktürk Empire was founded on the Orkhon River by gathering eight Turkish tribes, including the Uyghurs, the Oghuz, the Onoq and the Qarluqs (Karluk). By the middle of the sixth century they were living under the sovereignty of the Avars or Juan-Juan, under the leadership of Bumin. Bumin was given the title of "Khan" by the Göktürk State Council in recognition of his defeat of the Juan-Juan state in 552. Bumin Khan made

Ötüken his capital city. Ötüken was a holy city for Turks. Bumin Khan gave the western region of the empire to his brother Istemi, with the title of Yabghu. Istemi Yabghu was dependent on the Eastern Göktürks in external affairs, but had a free hand in internal affairs. Bumin Khan died at the end of the same year and was succeeded by his son Mukhan, in whose time the Göktürk Empire was really built on a grand scale. Mukhan swept the remnants of the Juan-Juan away to Europe, and brought the Kyrgyz, the Turkish tribes, the Kitans, and the Mongolic tribes under his control.

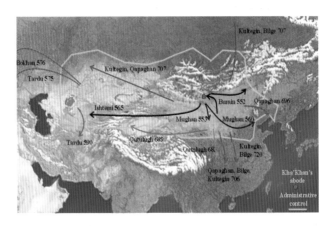

Istemi Yabghu also expanded his sovereignty from west of the Altai Mountains to Lake Issik and the Tien Shan Mountains. Then he initiated diplomatic contact with the Byzantine Empire and the Sassanids. First, Istemi Yabghu defeated the Ak-Huns with the collaboration of the Sassanids. Istemi Yabghu then made an alliance with Byzantium against the Sassanids, who had been after the control of the Silk Road. The control of the Silk Road had been a matter of intense rivalry between the Byzantines, the Sassanids, and the Göktürks. During Istemi's time the empire's western boundary expanded up to Crimea on the northern coast of the Black Sea.

The Göktürks reached their peak of power in the east with Istemi Yabghu, and in west with Mukan Khan. Although the dual ruling system was working quite well during Mukan's and Istemi's time, after their deaths the system of dual leadership became a weak point for the Göktürks as it created rivalry among the eastern and western Khanates and gave an opportunity to the Sui and Tang Dynasties of China to successfully played them against each other. Tardu, Istemi's son, who had already declared himself independent of the Khan after his father's death, did not assent to Ishpara (İşpara) Khan in the east, and caused a civil war which led the Göktürk Empire to split into an eastern and a western half in 582. Following his unsuccessful campaign, Ishpara became China's vassal in 585. Although successive Khans struggled for freedom, the eastern Göktürks were conquered by China in 630.

## Disintegration of the Göktürks

Having saved their freedom, the western Göktürks endeavored to re-establish the Göktürks' confederation and to expand their boundaries towards the West. Some considerable successes were obtained by Tardu (576-603). His achievements disturbed the Chinese however, who provoked a civil war in order to fend off Tardu's campaign. Afterwards the Turkish tribes, particularly the Töles (Tiele), rebelled against Tardu, who could not overcome these rebellions. Then in 603 Tardu himself took refuge with the Tu-yu-huns, a Mongolic tribe which created a chaotic atmosphere in the western Göktürk state until 611. During the reigns of She-koei Khan (611- 618) and Tong Yabghu (618-630), the Göktürks recovered some of their previous power by regaining control over the Töles who had expanded from the Orkhun Rivers to Lake Aral. By 630 the Göktürk's power began to diminish however, due to tribal rebellions and wars with the Chinese. The Chinese subjugated western portions of the Göktürk state in 659.

Thus, in the period spanning from 630 to 680, the Göktürks were subdued by the Chinese. Fifty years under Chinese control had a bad effect on the Turkish people, who began to examine the reasons why they lost their state and their spirit. According to the Orkhon inscriptions, the reasons for the defeat of the first Göktürk Empire were: an unwise Khan succeeded to the throne with incompetent high officials, the inappropriate attitude of the Turkish people and the wily and deceitful attitudes of the Chinese.

# Resurrection of the Göktürks

The Turks eventually turned against the Chinese with several uprisings from 679 to 681. These uprisings were led by heroic figures such as Kurshat. While these uprisings were unsuccessful in achieving their immediate aims, they provoked a national awakening among the Turks. Salvation came in the person of Kutluk, a descendant of the Ashina tribe, whose success in mobilizing the remnants of the scattered Turkish people led to the founding a second Göktürk Empire that lasted from 681 to 745.

Kutluk was given the title of Ilterish. He arranged several campaigns against some Turkish and alien tribes, as well as against the Chinese, in order to strengthen the economic and political position of the Göktürks. When he died in 692, the Turkish and alien tribes who had settled in the Khentei Mountains in the north, along the Onon and Kerulen rivers in the east, and in the Altai Mountains in the west, were brought under the Göktürks' sovereignty. Kapgan (692-716), the son of Kutluk, continued to pursue his father's policy of unifying the Turks of Asia under the Göktürk Flag. As part of this policy he tried to dominate China in order to bring in the Turks who were within Chinese borders. To achieve this goal, Kapgan Khan conducted twenty raids against garrisons in the north of China. Facing Turkish threats, the Chinese made an alliance with the Kyrgyz and the Onoqs in 696 and provoked the Turgish, the Qarluq, and many others to turn against the Göktürks. Kapgan responded ruthlessly against these Turkish tribes. This was a huge mistake on Kapgan's part, because some of them might have been peacefully persuaded to cease hostilities against the Göktürks. Instead, they became Kapgan's most bitter enemies. The Chinese took great advantage of this situation. Consequently, Kapgan was killed by the Bayirku (one of the Turkish tribes) with Chinese help. The Turgish claimed their independence and the Uyghurs were taken under Chinese control. Kapgan's successor, Inel Kagan, was not capable of coping with the situation. He was overthrown by Bilge Khan and Kül Tigin, the sons of Ilterish.

When Bilge Khan (meaning "wise khan") ascended to the throne (716-734), Kül Tigin was appointed commander of the Göktürk army, and Tonyukuk was appointed vizier. Following the advice of Tonyukuk, Bilge Khan and Kül Tigin professed that a khanate could not be ruled by means of war and bravery alone - they also recognized wisdom to be very important.

Therefore, Bilge Kagan did not initially arrange any campaigns against China. Instead, he gave priority to making domestic reforms, including re-establishing friendly relationships with the Turkish tribes, which had deteriorated in Kapgan's time. Meanwhile, the Chinese made alliances in 720 with the Turkish tribes of Kitan and Basmils for the purpose of waging war against the Göktürks. Bilge Khan averted the Chinese plan with the advice of his vizier, Tonyukuk. The Kitan and the Basmils were defeated before they could unite with the Chinese troops. Bilge Khan then turned on China and forced it to sign an agreement in 724, by which it consented to establishing a common market on the Chinese-Turkish frontier. This agreement produced notable economic advantages for the Göktürks.

Tonyukuk died in 725. Some scholars have called him "the Bismarck of the Göktürks" because of the crucial role he played in the domestic and foreign policies of the Göktürks. Kül Tigin died in 732 and Bilge Khan died in 734. After Bilge Khan's death, the Göktürks could not survive much longer in the face of an alliance made between the Qarluqs, the Basmils and the Uyghur in 745.

Bilge Khan and Kül Tigin are noted as the wisest and most heroic figures among Turkish statesmen in history. The first written texts of the Turkish language are inscriptions that immortalize the accomplishments of these khans and Tonyukuk.

### 3. The Uyghurs

The term "Uyhgur" was applied to a group of Turkish-speaking tribes that lived in the Altai Mountains. Along with the Göktürks, the Uyghurs were one of the largest and most enduring Turkish peoples living in Central Asia. According to Chinese records, the ancestors of the Uyghur were the Asian Huns. They were called "Kao-kü" during the Tabgach's time (386-534).

The Uyghurs established a principality in the valleys south of Lake Baikal and around the Yenisei River in the second half of the fifth century. Soon after, the Uygurs participated in a coalition with the Töles who dominated the northern part of Central Asia. In the first quarter of the seventh century, they took part in the coalition of six Syr-Tardush tribes. During Kapgan Khan's time, the Uygurs came under the Göktürks' sovereignty. Finally the Uyghur, together with other related subject tribes (the Basmil and the Qarluq), defeated the Göktürk Khanate and founded the Uyghur Empire at Mount Ötüken. The Uyghur Empire stretched from the Caspian Sea to Manchuria and lasted from 745 to 840. Its capital city was Ordu Baliq, built on the Orkhon River near where the Mongols later built Karakorum.

The Uyghur tribe that defeated the Göktürks consisted of the Doquz Urug (the meaning of "Urug" is not clear, but should refer to a large family). By eventually joining the Doquz-Oghuz, the Basmil and the Qarluqs constituted the Uyghur Empire. The first ruler of the Uyghur State was Kutluk Bilge Khan. When Kutluk died in 747, he was replaced by Moyunchur (747-759). During Moyunchur's reign there erupted the bitter struggle between the Arabs and the Chinese in Central Asia. This led to the Battle of Talas in 751, in which the Chinese were defeated. This provoked a civil war in China, who was forced to call the Uyghurs for help. Taking advantage of China's situation, the Uyghurs captured the Tarim basin. Although they could have conquered the Chinese Empire, the Uyghurs chose instead to use an exploitative trade policy to drain off the wealth of China without actually destroying it. Bögü Kagan maintained the same policy towards China. During his Chinese campaign, Bögü Kagan was so impressed by Manichaeism that he took four Manichaeist religious men back with him to the Uyghurs' territory. Consequently, the Uyghurs converted to Manichaeism in 762. This altered the Uyghurs' perception of life, as Manichaeism prohibited the eating of meat. This weakened the Uyghurs' spirit of belligerency.

In 840, following a famine and a civil war, the Uyghur Empire was overrun by the Kyrgyz, another Turkish people. As a result of this, the majority of tribal groups formerly under the umbrella of the Uyghurs migrated to Inner Asia.

Most of the Uyghurs departed from Ötüken and arrived in Kan-Chou (Kansu), where they met their kin who had been living there for 150 years. The newly arrived Uyghurs founded a state in 911 under the leadership of Tigin. Kan-Chou, who had control over important parts of the Silk Road, sent some delegations to China in order to establish friendly relationships based on trade. They had no remarkable military achievements, as they soon came under the Kitans in the tenth century and then under the Tanguts in the eleven century. In 1226 this area was dominated by the Mongols under Genghis Khan.

After their collapse, some other Uyghurs migrated to the Tien Shan Mountains, Besh Baliq, and the Turfan area where they founded a new state in 856 named the Turfan Uyghur State, or, the Eastern Uyghur State. The Turfan Uyghur State's sovereign was Mengly, the nephew of the last Uyghur Kagan in Ötüken. China needed a friendly neighbor as it was struggling with civil wars. The Eastern Uyghur state was also brought under Monghol control by Genghis Khan from 1209 to 1368, then Timur dominated the Uyghur region. Those who were descendants of the Timur or the Mongols maintained their authority over the region until the middle of the eighteenth century. After the middle of the nineteenth century, the Uyghurs' region became one of the strategic areas in which Great Britain, Russia, and China endeavored to expand their influence. Today a population of 10 million Uyghurs still lives the same region, which is under Chinese control.

## 4. The Turgish

The Turgish formed a part of the Tardush branch of the On-oq tribal Union (part of the western Göktürks). Their name first appeared in Chinese sources in 651, when they were living in the Ili Valley under the Göktürks' sovereignty. Following the defeat of the Göktürks, the Turgish managed to gain control of territories up to the provinces of Turfan and Kucha, and brought all the Onoq tribes under their control. These feats were accomplished under the leadership of Ushyly, who was given the title of "Baga Tarkan". At the peak of his reign, Ushyly Kagan decided to ally with the Chinese and the Kyrgyz to stop the expansionist Göktürks, who had reorganized and became powerful under Kapgan Kagan. Ushyly was defeated and taken prisoner however, at the Battle of Bolchu in 698 by Tonyukuk, the commander of the Göktürk army. Consequently, the Turgish became vassals of the Göktürks.

The second defeat of the Turgish by the Göktürks came in about 711 near Bolchu. Soko, the son of Ushyly, allied once again with China. Before the battle with the Göktürks, Soko's brother Chemu had already rebelled against him and had fled to Kapgan Kagan. At this time the Turgish were already separated into two parts as the Orkhun Inscriptions stated: the Kara (Black) Turgish and the Sarı (Yellow) Turgish.

The Göktürks rule over the Turgish did not last long, as they became independent in 717. Selecting Chor Sulu as their new

Kagan, many Göktürk chiefs and nobles abandoned Bilge Kagan and entered into Sulu's service. Sulu moved his capital to Balasaghun, northwest of Talas. Talas was the place where Sulu stopped the Umawwid army from expanding into Central Asia. After several successful wars against Umawwid Arabic expansionism, a long term civil war erupted between the Kara and Sarı Turgish in 738. Both sides were eventually defeated and destroyed by another Turkish tribe, the Qarluq in 766.

## 5. The Kyrgyz

Although recent historical findings on the Kyrgyz date back to 203 B.C., there is no detailed record about their earlier history. The early Kyrgyz lived in the upper Yenisei River valley. In the sixth century they were under the rule of the Göktürks. As the Göktürks fell under Chinese control in the years 630-680, the Kyrgyz became an independent tribe. However, they once more became vassals of the Second Göktürk state, then of the Uyghurs in 758. In the seventh and eighth centuries they were first introduced to Islam by Arab traders who traveled along the Silk Road.

After defeating the Uyghurs in 840, the Kyrgyz made Ötüken their capital city. In 920 they were forced to move out from Ötüken by Khitan, and they went back to their earlier location. In 1207 the Kyrgyz dominion had shrunk as a result of the Mongol invasions. The Kyrgyz eventually migrated south.

## 6. The Qarluq (Karluk)

The Qarluq (or Karluk), which means "bulk of snow", were originally a nomadic Turkish tribe that settled in the district of Kara-Irtish and Tarbagatay, west of the Altai Mountains. The Qarluq formed a part of the Onoq union together with three other tribes. Over time, the Qarluq moved westward and became one of the components of the Göktürks. The Qarluq played an important role in the Uyghurs' and Basmils' defeat of the Göktürks in 745. Afterwards, most of the Qarluq saw the Uyghur khanate as their master.

The Qarluq took the side of the Arabs in Battle of Talas in 751. The Battle of Talas was fought by the Umawwid

Arabs and the Chinese Tang Dynasty over control of Transoxiana where the Turgish's authority had grown weaker. In 766 the Qarluq tribes formed a Khanate under the rule of a Yabgu after they overran the Turgish in the Talas area. Their capital was Balasaghun, while they remained loyal to the Uyghur. After the Uyghur's defeat, the Qarluq declared their independence. The Qarluq were the first Turkish people who converted to Islam and played an important role in establishing the Kara-Khanid (Karahanlı), the first Turkish Islamic state.

## 7. The Oghuz

The name Oghuz derives from the word "ok" which means "tribe" or "arrow" in Turkish. The letter "z" in the suffix makes the word plural in old Turkish grammar. "Okuz" later in the sixth century changed to "Oguz" (Oghuz), or "Uz", as stated in Byzantine sources. When they were under the Göktürks' rule, the Oghuz were named Üç (three) Oghuz or Sekiz (eight) Oghuz, but mostly Dokuz (nine) Oghuz, and later On (ten) Oghuz. During the establishment of the Göktürk state, the Oghuz tribes inhabited the Altai Mountain region and also the area along the Tula River. They were also present as a community near the Barlik River. During the Göktürks' time, the Oghuz grew larger as various other Turkish tribes united with them. Therefore, the designation of "Oghuz" was given to a series of Turkish nomadic or semi-nomadic tribes in Central Asia who had united into a new tribal confederation (bodun).

Following the collapse of the Göktürks, the Oghuz came under the Uyghur. In the time of Moyunchur (747-759) some of the Oghuz fought against Uyghur authority, but they were defeated three times at the Selenga River. Then they may have come to Transoxiana towards the end of the eighth century. It is clear that they were living in the area spanning from east of the Caspian Sea to the Seyhun River (Syr-darya) in the tenth and eleventh centuries. They founded a state called Oghuz Yabghu in the first half of the tenth century with the Pechenegs and the Khazars as hostile neighbors. The relationship with the Qarluqs, the eastern neighbor of the Oghuz, was also hostile. These Oghuz called themselves "Turk" and also "Turkmen", which became the name of the Oghuz after they converted to Islam. Each confederation consisted of twelve tribes, which meant that the Oghuz confederation combined twenty four Turkish tribes. The Oghuz had been organized in a dual tribal confederation system in Oghuz Yabg'su's time that was known as the Üç-Ok. The Üç-Ok confederation included the Kınık Tribes (who later founded the Seljuk state) and the Boz-ok and Kayı tribes who founded the Ottoman state.

The Oghuz Yabghu state was defeated as the result of harassments by the Kypchak, the Khazar and the Qarluqs. Another factor for this defeat may have been leaving the Seljuk people with their groups from the Oghuz confederation in the west. Following the defeat the Oghuz Yabghu State, some Oghuz migrated westwards via the lands north of the Black Sea and reached the Balkans where they were renamed as "Uz". The Uz are the ancestors of the Gagavuzs in Romania. Some of the others (the Seljuk) headed towards Khorasan. Some of the Oghuz people remained in their homeland in the Altai Mountain region.

# CHAPTER 2

## Early Medieval Eastern European Turkish Tribes and States

### 1. The Western Huns

During the last two centuries scholars in different disciplines of the social sciences have advanced various theories about the origins of the Western Huns. Recent cultural and ethnographic sources have made it clear that the Western Huns were of Turkish origin, and that they were the descendents of the Asian Huns.

The northern Huns began to migrate towards the West at the beginning of the second century, where they re-united with the tribes of Chi-chi. Due to the pressure of nomadic tribes in the middle of the fourth century, the Huns began a massive migration westwards and reached the river Itil (Volga) in 374. As they advanced, they encountered two Germanic peoples settled along the northern shores of the Black Sea: the Ostrogoths, whom they overpowered, and the Visigoths, whom the Romans allowed to settle as a nation within the Roman Empire south of the Danube River in return for military service.

As the Huns encountered the Germanic peoples, a bitter struggle was unavoidable between the two nomadic groups. The Huns, under the command of Balamir (the first recorded chief of the western Huns) defeated the Ostrogots in 374. Hun attacks continued towards the West due to the astonishing ability of their cavalry troops. When they reached the Dnieper River in 375, Hun troops caused the Visigoths to collapse. The Visigoth king Atanarik fled with his troops towards Roman-controlled territory in the West at around the time (395) when the Roman Empire was divided into an Eastern and a Western Empire. Thus, the pressure exerted by Huns with their entry into Eastern Europe caused a huge fluctuation of the European population. Consequently, all people from East and Central Europe were ejected from their countries, which sparked an "immigration o f the tribes" that profoundly altered the ethnic composition of Europe.

A terror was awakened among the Eastern European tribes by the sudden and impetuous Hun attacks. The appearance of Hun raider squads in unexpected areas left a horrible impression on the Western world. Many Latin and Greek writers of the time expressed a profound hostility towards the Huns which in turn contributed to their excessive villainization in Western culture.

During the last decade of the fourth century the Huns conducted a series of raids on Anatolia and the Middle East, which ended in the raid on Jerusalem, via Caucasia, under the command of Basik and Kursik. The Eastern Roman Empire could not take any defensive measures against these raids. By 400 another Hun campaign under Uldiz's command against the Goths in the southern Danube region restarted a massive westward migration of the Goths. The Goths took refugee within the Roman Empire. The Romans were not pleased with these barbarians as they threatened the territorial integrity of the empire. The Romans pleaded with the Huns for support in their struggle against the Visigoths. This appeal was met by Uldiz, who defeated Radagais, the commander of the Goths. During Uldiz's rule, the Huns developed a foreign policy that would be followed until the end of Attila's time. This foreign policy dictated the lending of support to strong powers against weaker powers. Accordingly, the Huns established friendly relations with the Western Roman Empire while they put strong pressure on the Byzantines against whom the Huns gained a series of victories. As part of this policy, the Huns took part in the Western Romans' effort to fend off both the Visigothic and Byzantine attacks. Taking advantage of the four-year-old Valentinianus who was ascending to the throne, Theodious sent an army and navy to Italy in order to take possession of Rome. To thwart Theodious, the Western Roman state requested that Rua, the Chief of the Huns, arrange an expedition to Italy with 60 thousand cavalry. Theodious could not venture into war with the Huns, but still had to pay a tribute of 350 Roman pounds to the Huns. Theodious II's attitude towards the Huns remained hostile.

By 432 the Huns were united under Rua. Following his death in 434, his nephews Attila and Bleda were left in control of all the united Hun tribes. At the time of their accession the Huns were bargaining with Theodious II's envoys over the return of several renegade tribes who had taken refuge within the Byzantine Empire. The Byzantine Empire signed of an agreement that consented to certain terms put forward by the Huns at Margus. The Byzantines agreed not only to return the fugitive tribes, but also to double their previous tribute and to open their markets to Hunnic traders. Yet as Theodious dawdled over applying the terms of the agreement, Attila initiated a war against the Byzantines through Thrace. Aetius, the commander of the Western Roman army, prevented this war by guaranteeing that Theodious would apply the terms of the agreement. Nothing had changed on Theodious' side. This time he went one step further by planning to assassinate Attila in 448, who had taken charge after Bleda's death in 445. The plan was unsuccessful as the assassin was captured before his attempt. A frightening atmosphere prevailed over the Byzantine capital as Attila's furious might caused mortal conflict. Realizing the threat, Theodious II did not delay in making his apology. Luckily, he escaped from imminent catastrophe as Attila, who believed Byzantine was not an immediate threat for the Huns, gave his priority to the Western Roman question, to which Attila arranged a two-year political and military campaign.

In 450 the emperor Valentinian III's sister Honoria sent Attila an engagement ring in order to escape her forced betrothal to a Roman senator. Attila saw this proposal as a great opportunity to ask for half of the western Empire as a dowry. When Valentinian III discovered the plan, only the influence of his mother convinced him to exile Honaria rather than to kill her. He wrote to Attila strenuously denying the legitimacy of the supposed marriage proposal. Attila, not convinced, sent an envoy to Valentinian III to proclaim that the proposal had been legitimate, and that he would come to claim what was rightfully his.

The Western question was not limited to this marriage. A succession struggle between the two sons of the King of the Salian Franks drove a rift between Attila and Aetius: Attila supported the elder son, while Aetius, the de facto ruler, supported the younger. Attila proclaimed his intention to attack the Visigoths who had made an alliance with Valentinian III against the Vandals, who in turn were seeking Hun support. Attila's main interest was to prevent the Romans from gaining superiority over the western tribes who were accepting

Christianity, which became the Romans Empire's official religion in 330. As early as 451, Attila gathered two hundred thousands troops (including his Slavic and Germanic vassals) and moved as far west as Orleans. Aetius moved to oppose him with the Burgundians and Visigoths under King Theodoric I. The two armies clashed in the Battle of Chalons, whose outcome is in a matter of discussion among historians. However, the fact that the Western tribes were not in a position, as the result of the war, to help the Romans in 452 in a war between Valentinian and Attila shows that Attila was the victor.

Believing that the Romans were not in a position to gather any troops from the western tribes, Attila initiated a final campaign with one hundred thousand troops against Valentinian by re-claiming his marriage to Honoria. He arrived in Rome by passing through Venice, whose residents fled to small islands in the Venetian Lagoon. A frightening climate permeated Rome. Aetius did not have the courage to meet Attila. Finally a Roman delegation, including Trigetius, the Consul Aviennus and Pope Leo I, pleaded with Attila for forgiveness. This plea was accepted by Attila. Peace conditions were established and Attila turned his army back, having achieved nothing.

Several explanations for his actions have been put forwarded: the declaration of Rome's surrender was seen as enough by Attila, believing that no further threat would be launched against the Huns by Rome. The new Byzantine Emperor Marcian's campaign against the Huns might have also influenced Attila's withdrawal. Whatever his reasons, Attila left Italy and returned to his palace across the Danube. He planned a campaign to the East but he died in the early months of 453.

Attila had three sons: Ilek (Ellak), Dengizik (Dengizich) and Irnek (Ernakh). None of them possessed Attila's charismatic leadership. Ilek was the first to sit on the throne, but he was defeated and died in a battle with Germanic tribes at Nedao in 454. Dengizik's effort for unification was a failure because of his defeat by the Byzantine Empire in 469. Irnek realized that the scattered Huns could not survive in Central Europe. So he took the remnants of the Huns to the western coast of the Black Sea, stretching from the mouth of Danube to the Volga River. There they met with the Ogur tribes, who came from east of the Ural Mountains as the result of Sabar harassment.

## 2. The Avar Khanate

The Avars were one of the nomadic Turkish people of Eurasia. They were one of the successors of the Turkish states of the Huns in Central Asia. Chinese sources indicate that the Avars identified with Jaun-Juan (Rouran) and were driven westwards by the Göktürks in 552. They later appeared in Central and Eastern Europe following their victory over the Sabars in 557. Their rule over much of Central Europe lasted into the early ninth century. Then they pushed north into Germany, as Attila had done a century before, eventually reaching as far north as the Baltic Sea. The Avars then turned their attention to the Pannonian plain which was being contested by various Germanic tribes (the Lombards and the Gepids). After defeating them, the Avars established a state in the Danube River area. Avar harassment forced the Lombards to move into northern Italy, which marked the last Germanic mass movement in the migration period.

In 626, the Avars besieged but failed to capture Istanbul (Constantinople). Following this event, the Avars retreated to their center. They lost control of the Balkans to Slavic tribes. Most of the Avars' subjects became independent, with the exception of those in Pannonia. Internal and external pressure started to undermine the Avar state by the early ninth century. They were finally liquidated by the Frankish king Charlemagne (Charles the Great) in 805. The Avars were later assimilated into the indigenous populations of central Europe, mainly into the Hungarian population.

## 3. The Sabars

Though their earlier history is not well-known, the Sabars were one of the Turkish people that lived under the sovereignty of the Asian Hun Empire. The Sabars' fatherland was the area stretching from the east of the Tien Shan Mountains to the Ili River. They formed one of the Turkish states that dominated Western Siberia and Northern Caucasia in the fifth and sixth centuries. They migrated to the West due to the pressures of the Avars in the second half of the fifth century. They settled in the Volga-Don basin at the beginning of sixth century. In the Volga-Don basin they constituted a powerful political and military state. During this time the Sabars allied with Sassanids and fought against the Byzantines. The Sabars advanced into central

Anatolia. The Sabars' forces were weakened however, after the Avar's second attack in 557. Shortly afterwards they became one of the Göktürks' components. The Sabars formed the main component of the Hazar state in the seventh century.

## 4. The Hazar (Khazar) Khanate

The Khazars were a semi-nomadic Turkish people from Central Asia. Before their migration to the west, the Khazars were one of the Turkish tribes living under the rule of the Asian Huns. Soviet scholars considered the Khazars to be the indigenous people of the Northern Caucasus. The Khazars were related to the Ashina tribes, the founders of the first Göktürk Empire. After the collapse of the first Göktürk Empire, the Khazars joined a tribal confederation in the west led by the Ashina tribes. The Khazars' state organization resembled that of the Göktürks.

The Khazars' first significant appearance in history is at the beginning of the seventh century when they aided the campaign of the Byzantine emperor Heraclius against the Sassanids. The Khazars saved Byzantium from defeat. From the seventh to the ninth centuries the Khazars had friendly relations with the Byzantine Empire. During this time the Khazars had serious conflicts with the Umawwid Abbasid Caliphates and hindered their expansion over Caucasia by forming a united front with the remnants of the Göktürks in Transoxiana. The Khazars flourished in the Caspian Sea, in the area north of the Black Sea, and in Eastern Europe. In Eastern Europe, the Khazars brought together several tribes who had already been living there. When Khazaria became a major regional power the Byzantines abandoned their alliance with the Khazars. The Byzantines then turned to the Russia (the proto-Russians) and the Pechenegs to form an alliance against the Khazars. In 965 the Khazars were conquered by the Rus' of Kiev.

The Khazar royalty and nobility converted to Judaism in the last decades of the eighth century and the early ninth century. A part of the general Khazar population also converted to Judaism. Another significant portion of the Khazar population also converted to Islam and to Christianity.

## 5. The Pechenegs

After the Göktürks' defeat, the Pechenegs, who were one of the Göktürks' subjects, moved westwards. The Pechenegs dominated the area between the lower Volga, the Don and Diniester by the ninth century. The Pechenegs did not succeed in founding a state, instead they remained a tribal confederation. As a tribal confederation the Pechenegs played a crucial role in world history by pushing the Oghurs from the Asov Sea into Central Europe (into present day Hungary). The Pechenegs provoked the movement of the Finno-Ugric tribes into Europe. The Pechenegs also prevented the Russians from entering the Black Sea for a long time. The Pechenegs raided Russian lands many times. After a long alliance, the Pechenegs began to harass the Byzantines. In 1091 the Pechenegs were defeated by an alliance of Kyphaks and Byzantines. They did not recover from this defeat.

## 6. The Kypchaks

The most powerful and multitudinous tribe of the last massive migrations was the Kypchak. The time of the Kypchaks' first appearance in history is unclear. However, it is thought that their history may date back to the end of the eighth or early ninth century in East Central Asia. They became neighbors of the Oghuz when the Kharahitay forced them to move west. The Kypchaks grew in number and they allied with the Kimek People. They began to harass the Oghuz and affected their migration to the West. Then they struggled against the Russian principalities. Consequently, the Kypchaks dominated the area from the Caspian Sea to the southern Ukraine. This area was called the "Kypchaks' steppe". The Kypchaks invaded Moldavia, Walachia, and part of Transylvania in the eleventh century, and they began to plunder the Byzantine Empire and the Kingdom of Hungary. In 1239 the Kypchaks were defeated by the Mongol invaders at the Battle of Khalka. After the breakup of the Mongol Empire, the Kypchaks who remained in their land comprised a significant portion of the Golden Horde. The Kypchaks established a presence in parts of present day Russia, the Ukraine, and Kazakhstan. They played a significant role in turkifying the Mongols.

## 7. The Ogur and the Bulgarian States

The Oghur were of the same origins as the Oghuz, they were one of the main Turkish tribal confederations. Western sources called those who migrated west by way of the northern Tien Shan Mountains the "Oghur". They settled in the northern Black Sea area and formed a separated tribal union, as the Oghuz had done. The Ogurs' tribal union consisted of the Dokuz-Ogur in the steppes of the Dnieper area, the On-Ogur in Northern Caucasia, and the Otuz-Ogur in the area between the Don and the Volga. The Ogur in the West were brought under the Göktürks in 576. When the Göktürk Empire collapsed in 630, the On-Ogur founded Great Bulgaria in northern Caucasia under the Chieftainship of Kurt. Kurt originated from the Asian Huns, and he allied himself with Byzantium. Great Bulgaria came under Khazar sovereignty in 665. Soon after, the Ogurs moved to the Balkans north of the Danube under the leadership of Asparuh, the son of Kurt. In the Balkans they founded the Tuna Bulgarian State in 679 in the area south of present day Dobrudzha (Dobruca).

The Tuna Bulgarian State established good relationships with the Byzantines. The Tuna Bulgarians defended Constantinople when the Umawwid Arabs besieged it in 717-718. Consequently, the Bulgarians gained economic advantages and secured their eastern boundaries. However, this did not last long as the Byzantines attacked Bulgaria during an internal struggle for the Bulgarian throne in the middle of the eighth century.

In 814 the Byzantines found themselves in a difficult position as Krum Khan besieged Constantinople. Fortunately for the Byzantines, Krum Khan suddenly died. Under the leadership of Krum Khan's son, Omurtag Khan (814-831), Bulgaria reached its peak in every respect. During this time the Turkish population of the Tuna Bulgarian state began to lose its identity due to the mass influx of Slavic peoples. When the Bulgarian state was converted to Orthodox Christianity in 864 by Boris (852-889), the Tuna Bulgarians moved away from Turkish cultural practices and adopted Slavic ones.

Another state that was established after collapse of Great Bulgaria was the Itil (Volga) Bulgarian state. The Volga Bulgarian state was founded in the vicinity of the Itil and Kama rivers. Its capital city was Bulgar, which was the main trading center in Eastern Europe from the ninth to the twelfth centuries. The Volga Bulgarian state converted to Islam in 922. Some historians claim that it was the first Turkish state to enter Islam. The Volga Bulgarians were defeated in 1237 by the Mongols. The Volga Bulgarians belonged to the Golden Horde until the middle of the fifteenth century.

The course of Turkish history began to change when the Turks met the Muslim states of Umayyad and Abbasid on their westward migrations towards the Middle East and Anatolia. Through these encounters the Turks gradually began to convert to Islam.

# CHAPTER 3

## The First Turkish Muslim States

The Turks' conversion to Islam can be analyzed from social, historical, and political angles. However, from whatever angle it is approached, this event is of great importance. When handled in socio-economic terms, the change of religion is probably one of the most important events a person or nation comes face to face in his/her/its life. When the issue is taken in terms of the life of a nation, the change of religion has direct effects on the social, the political, and even the economic structures of that nation. In this regard, the Turks' conversion to Islam produced important changes in Turkish history and, as all other truly monumental events, it changed the course of world history. When handled in historical terms, this event can be recognized as a turning point in Turkish history that demarcates it into two stages - a pre-Islamic stage, and an Islamic stage. The conversion to Islam signaled the beginning of Turkish Islamic History. Finally, when viewed from a political standpoint, it formed the basis of a new era in Turkish History that continued until the twentieth century.

The Turks did not become familiar with Islam during the lifetime of the Prophet Mohammed, and thus they did not have the opportunity to become familiar with it directly through the Prophet. The Turks' relationship with Muslim Arabs began in the period of the second Caliph Omar. The Turks first came face to face with Islam when they helped the Persians fight against the invading Islamic armies. This first contact did not make them instant converts. The first development that caused the Turks to know Islam was the Islamic armies' conquest of Persia in the middle of the seventh century. In 651 the Islamic armies began their expedition towards Persia. They passed the Amu Darya (Ceyhun) River that was recognized as the Turkish border, and eventually they conquered Transoxiana in 705. Due to the bad administration of the Umayyad in this region, the Turkish rulers did not let the Umayyad Islamic armies precede easily. The Turgish Khanate waged a particularly successful struggle against the Umayyads.

In 750 the administration of the Islamic state passed into the hands of the Abbasids. At this point there began a new stage in Turkish-Arab relations. In Transoxiana, while the Turk-Arab fight continued, some of the Turkish groups asked for help from China. Seeing this as a great opportunity to dominate Turkmenistan, China sent a great army to the west in 747. The crude attitudes of the Chinese in this region however, caused the Turks to detach themselves from this force. The Turks asked for help from the Khorasan governor of the Islamic state against the Chinese. The governor Ebu Muslim accepted this request for help and sent an army against the Chinese. In July 751, the Chinese and the Islamic-supported Turks fought in the surroundings of today's Almaty on the side of the Talas River. The Chinese were resoundingly defeated in this conflict, which is known as the Talas War.

The Talas War became a milestone in Turkish history. After this war the strife between the Arabs and the Turks ended. Good relations were established between the two sides. The war period ended and the peace period began. In this peace period, commercial relations developed between the two nations and as a result, the Turks had the opportunity to gain a better knowledge of the Islamic religion. This caused the spread of Islam among the Turks. Before accepting the Islamic religion, the Turks believed in various other religions, such as Manichaeism, Buddhism, and Zoroastrianism. In this regard, changing religion was not something foreign to them. However, none of these religions were adopted with such an overwhelming majority as Islam.

During the Umayyad period, the Turks' acceptance of Islam remained confined to scattered groups of individuals. In the Abbasid period, Islam widened its area of influence and began to be accepted on a massive level. The more moderate policy of the Abbasids towards the non-Arab Muslims played an important role in this process. From the ninth century onwards, a massive Islamization process was seen among the Turkish groups. These groups first served the Islamic State, but later they founded independent states and gradually became so powerful as to be able to decide the fate of the Islamic world as a whole.

## 1. The Kara-Khanid Khanate (840 - 1212)

The Kara-Khanid Khanate was founded by the Yaghma, Cigil and Tohsi clans in 840. The founding of the Kara-Khanid Khanate came after the Uyghur state was destroyed by the Kyrgyz, and the Qarluq Yabghu declared itself to be the sole and lawful descendant of the master of the steppes. In 893 it became the Centrum of the Kashgar state. To this first Islamic state that ruled in western and eastern Turkistan the name "Kara-Khanid" was given by European orientalists. This name was derived from the word "Kara" (strong) that was often used as a title among the people of this state. For instance, when the Qarluq Yabghu declared itself as the master of the steppes, it used the title Kara Khan.

The Kara-Khanid Khanate, in accordance with the traditional structure of Turkish states, was divided into two parts -a right and a left. The Great Khan who was the ruler of the whole state was situated in the east/right part. In the left part of the state was situated the second person in command, who should have been called "yabghu", but due to the khan title used in the state was instead called "dependent khan." The autonomous provinces that existed in both parts were administered by the Sultan's sons or military governors who were dependent on the dynasty. After the Kara-Khanid Khanate was divided into an eastern and a western part, the tradition of having a separate administration in each part continued to exist. No information was recorded in historical texts on the Great Khans situated in the eastern part. The only recorded information on this state comes from the western secondary khans, who had good contact with the Islamic world and who presided over the most basic state affairs. When the history of the state is investigated one sometimes experiences incertitude about the head of the state.

In the initial period of the Khanid Khanate (which was not well-documented) the first recorded ruler was Bilge Kül Kadir Khan. The only information recorded on Bilge Kül Kadir Khan concerns his struggle with the Samanids. After Bilge Kül Kadir Khan, his sons Ogulcak Kadir Khan and Bazir Arslan Khan governed the state. The nephew of Ogulcak Kadir Khan, Satik Bughra, came to power after he defeated his uncle in a bid for the throne. Satık Bughra made Islam the official religion in the provinces he dominated. In the time of Satık Bughra (who adopted the name "Abdulkerim" after becoming Muslim) the Islamic religion spread rapidly among the Turkish clans. During the reigns of Satık Bughra Khan's successors (especially that of Baytash Arslan Khan Suleyman) Islam prevailed over the whole of the country. That is to say, from the 960s onwards the Kara-Khanid Khanate can be said to have continued its life as a Turkish Muslim State.

In its political history, the Kara-Khanid Khanate fought with the Samanids, the Ghaznavids, and in later periods with the

Seljuks. In the time of Kılıç Bughra Khan, the Samanid state was destroyed and the Transoxiana region was conquered. However, the Khanids did not succeed in taking Khorasan from the Ghaznavids. After it enlarged its domination to many regions in the 1030s, power struggles began inside the Khanate and this situation led to the division of the country into two independent states in 1042: the Western and Eastern Khanates. The Western Kara-Khanids dominated the regions from Transoxiana to Fergana. The center of the Western Khanate was first Özkent and later Samarkand. This state became incorporated into the Great Seljuk Empire in 1074. When the Seljuks were defeated by the Karahitays, it passed into the hands of the victors. In 1212 the Harzemshahs ended the life of this state.

The political and military center of the Western Kara-Khanid Khanate was Balasagun, and its cultural and religious center was Kashgar. The Khanate dominated the regions of Balasagun, Talas, Tashkent, Kashgar, Yarkent, and Hotan. They struggled to spread Islam among the non-Muslim Turks in the eastern part of the state. In 1089 it passed into the hands of the Great Seljuk Empire and was destroyed in 1211 by the Karahitays. Apart from the Western and Eastern Kara-Khanid Khanates, a third Kara-Khanid Khanate was founded in 1141. This third Khanate was known as the Fergana Khanate, its center was Ozkent. The Fergana Khanate disappeared in 1212.

## 2. The Ghaznavid Empire (963 - 1187)

The Ghaznavid Empire was a Turkish Islamic state founded in 963 in Afghanistan. The empire took its name from Ghazna, the city where it was founded. The Ghaznavid Empire had an important place among the first Turkish Islamic States as it became an important regional power, especially in northern India.

In the ninth and tenth centuries the Turks had begun to participate and serve in the Islamic states. Over time they became an elite group of governors and commanders in those states. Those who founded the Ghaznavid State were Turks who previously served the Samanid State. During the Samanid state's disintegration, Alptegin was one of the commanders of the Samanid State who was appointed governor of Khorasan. Bel'ami, the Samanid vizier of the time, challenged Alptegin for supremacy of the Samanid state, but was unsuccessful. Alptegin defeated the army sent against him. Alptegin then came to the city of Ghazna in Afghanistan and drove away the native Leviks from the region in 962. He began to dominate the city, and in 963 he declared himself ruler of the region and founded the Ghaznavid Empire.

In the time of Alptegin's successor Ebu Ishak Ibrahim, Ghazna was retaken by the Leviks. Soon after it was taken back by the Ghaznavids. Since Ebu Ishak Ibrahim had no son, the administration of the state passed into the hands of his commanders. Bilge Tegin, who was the first of these commanders, declared his dependency on the Samanids. After Bilge Tegin, Bori Tegin came to power. Having complained about the bad administration of Bori Tegin, the Ghaznavids invited the Leviks to dominate the city. Another commander, Sebüktigin, first prevented the Leviks from entering the city; then, overthrowing Bori Tegin from power, he himself became the ruler in 977. Though Sebüktigin was independent in his region, he accepted the domination of the Samanids.

After Sebuktigin came to power an important change occurred in the administration of the Ghaznavid State. Until then, the State had been administered by commanders. Under Sebuktigin's governorship, the administrative system was changed into a dynasty. Sebuktigin must have thought that the best way to preserve the state was to dynamically enlarge its borders, because as soon as he came to power and changed the administrative system he began expanding the lands of the Empire. In a short time, the borders of the Ghaznavid Empire were enlarged to include Toharistan, Zabulistan, Zemindaver, Gur and Belucistan. Later Sebuktigin sent a military expedition towards India to also include that region in the borders of the Empire. With this first Turkish Islamic movement against the northern Indian Princes (the Rajas), Sebüktigin played an important role in spreading Islam as far as Peshaver (in northern India). He also assisted his son Mahmut in repressing the Samanids' rebellion in the Khorasan region. To reward his services, the Samanid State gave him the title "Nair al-din," (The Spreader of Religion) and appointed his son Mahmut to the Khorasan governorship. When Sebuktigin died in 997 in Ghazna, his son Mahmut became his successor.

Mahmut became an important figure not only for the Ghaznavid Empire, but also for Turkish history. He was the first ruler to use the title of Sultan. At the beginning of his leadership Mahmut had a power struggle with his brother. During this familial power struggle the Samanids invaded Khorasan and appointed a governor to the region. After he defeated his brother and made his domination in the State certain, Mahmut asked the Samanid ruler to leave Khorasan. As his demand was rejected by the Samanids, he invaded Khorasan. The Samanid State was so weakened after losing Khorasan that the Kara-Khanid Khanate eventually came to an end. As a consequence of the end of the Kara-Khanid Khanate, the Ghaznavids became totally independent.

The first job of Sultan Mahmut was to sign a treaty with the Kara-Khanids. With this treaty, the Samanid lands were shared and the Northern part of the State was made secure against foreign invasions. Sultan Mahmut then captured Sistan, Huttal, and Khwarezm. After this series of victories, he sent military expeditions to India. Those expeditions had two aims: to spread Islam in India and to seize riches. To achieve these aims Sultan Muhmut completed 17 expeditions to India between the years 1001 and 1027. Through these expeditions Sultan Mahmut expanded the dominion of the Turks over the whole of northern India, including the Pencap, the Indus, the Und, the Moltan, the Tanisar, the Lokhot, the Gwalior, and the Somnat regions. With these expeditions the spread of Islam reached a massive level in northern India. Th e foundations of today's Pakistan were also established. Mahmut gained great prestige in the Islamic world. He was one the greatest rulers in Turkish Islamic History. When Sultan Mahmut came to power the Ghaznavid State was a small principality. By the time of his death in 1030 the Ghaznavid State had become an empire whose borders expanded in the west to Azerbaijan, in the east to the Ganges vale of India, and in middle-Asia from Khwarezm to the Indian Ocean.

In the power struggle that occurred between Mahmut's sons after his death, Mesut defeated his brother Muhammed and became Mahmut's successor. Mesut was as successful as his father in the administration of the Empire. During Mesut's reign the army of the Great Seljuk Empire attempted to invade Khorasan and began to pose a great threat for the Ghaznavids. The Ghaznavids were eventually defeated in the Battle of Dandanaqan by the Seljuks. With this defeat the Ghaznavids had to withdraw to India, after having already lost Khorasan, Khwarezm, and all the regions in the north. Mesut was murdered in a rebellion during the withdrawal. The Ghaznavids could not reorganize after these events. Ibrahim, who became the Sultan in

1059, accepted Seljuk domination. This dependency on the Seljuks continued until the Seljuks were defeated by the Karahitays in the Battle of Kat van. As the Seljuk domination ended in Ghazna, the Afghan Ghorid Alauddin captured the city. In 1187 the Ghorids also captured the new center of Lahor and killed its last ruler, Husrev Melik. The Ghorids ended the Ghaznavid Empire.

The Ghaznavid Empire holds an important place in Turkish Islamic history because of its daring expeditions to India that contributed to the spread of Islam.

# CHAPTER 4

## The Great Seljuk Empire

The Great Seljuk Empire was founded by the Oghuz Turks, also known as the Kınık Seljuks. The Empire got its name from Seljuk Bey. Seljuk Bey was a commander (*subaşı*) in the Oghuz Yabghu State who migrated to the Cend region with the clans under his rule and founded the Seljuk State. Seljuk Bey's father, Dukak, was also a commander in the Oghuz Yabghu State. His son Seljuk became commander upon his death. As he departed from the Yabghu, he immigrated with the clans to the south: to the Cend region on the side of the Syr-Darya River. Another reason for this migration, as in all the migrations in Turkish history, was the inadequacy of the dwelling and grazing lands to meet the needs of the growing population.

The Seljuks' arrival in Cend marked the beginning of an important period in history. Cend had been inhabited by Muslims who had immigrated from Transoxiana and a border city between the Turks and the Islamic countries. In this period many Turkish clans had already converted to Islam. Seljuk however, was not yet a Muslim. Seljuk brought Islamic religious guides to Cend from the surrounding Islamic countries such as Bukhara and Khwarezm (Harezm). These religious guides made Seljuk's habitation in Cend more favorable to the locals. In 960 Seljuk converted to Islam together with the Oghuzs living under his rule. These Islamicized Oghuzs began to be called "Turkmen". This name was later used for the Oghuzs who migrated to Muslim countries.

After accepting Islam, Seljuk gradually became powerful in the region. He decided to cut his political ties with the Yabghu and sent back tax collectors from the Oghuz Yabghu by saying: "I do not pay taxes to non-Muslims." With this attitude he showed himself to be a veteran ready to fight for Islam. For this reason, he was given the title *El-Melikul Ghazi*. This posed two important advantages for Seljuk: first, he obtained the support of many Muslims and made the Turks join him; second, he diminished the dominance of the Yabghu around him and established an independent administration. As the Seljuk State became powerful it became recognized by neighboring countries as a major force in the international arena. The Seljuks were held in such high esteem by their neighbors that when the Samanids and the Kara-Khanids were fighting each other, the Samanids asked the Seljuks for help. The Samanids defeated the Kara-Khanids with the help of the Seljuks. They rewarded the Seljuks for their help by giving them as their hometown Nur, between Bukhara and Samarkand in 985. In future decades the Seljuks continued to play an important role in the struggle between the Samanids and the Kara-Khanids.

Seljuk Bey died when he was about 100 years old in Cend. Seljuk Bey's successor was Arslan, who came to power with the title Yabghu. Seljuk Bey's grandchildren, Tugrul and Çağrı (sons of Mikhail, who died in the lifetime of his father Seljuk Bey) took positions in the state administration with the title of *bey*. Tugrul and Çağrı Beys thought the future of the country should be sought in a wide area of land. Thus Tugrul moved towards deserts that were difficult to reach. His brother Çağrı conducted an expedition to eastern Anatolia with a chosen military force in 1016-1021. Çağrı's force was originally composed of five to six thousand soldiers, with more joining on the way as they passed through Khorasan. Çağrı came up against the Georgians and the Armenians in eastern Anatolia. He defeated them and saw that there was no force in the region that he and his soldiers could not defeat. This self-confidence led the Seljuks to make important political and military decisions. During this time, Arslan Yabghu and his successor Yusuf both died. Musa Inanc Yabghu became the new head of the Seljuks. However, the real power belonged to Tugrul Bey and Çağrı Bey. The eastern Anatolian expedition increased the importance of the two brothers to such an extent that the Ghaznavid Empire had begun to see the Seljuks as a threat.

In 1035 the Seljuks entered Khorasan without permission from the Ghaznavids ruling the city. The Seljuks took the scattered groups of Turkmens in Khorasan into their sphere of influence. When the Seljuks wanted the city to be given to them, the Ghaznavid sultan Mesut refused to concede. To expel the Seljuks from the city, sultan Mesut organized two military expeditions against the Seljuk State: one in 1035 and the other in 1038. The Seljuk State was successful in fighting off both expeditions. More importantly, the Seljuks understood that they could find support in Khorasan and remain there as a permanent power. Besides, in Khorasan a *khutba* (a collection of sacred congregational sermons delivered on the eve of Friday prayer) was read in the name of Tugrul Bey and the newly captured places that were distributed among his family members. After these developments, the Ghaznavid sultan Mesut took action to totally end the problem and headed with a great force towards Khorasan.

The two forces finally faced each other in the surroundings of the Dandanaqan castle. At the end of a battle that continued for three days (May 22-24, 1040) the Ghaznavids were very badly defeated. What made this battle important in history was its political consequences. The battle of Dandanaqan had become for the Seljuks a war of independence. The Seljuks had achieved their aim of founding an independent state in Khorasan. This had been an important goal ever since the Seljuks had first settled in Cend. After the battle, Tugrul Bey was declared Sultan (1040-1063) and the Seljuk Empire was officially established with its center in the city of Nishapur.

## The Rise of the Seljuk State

Tugrul Bey's first action as sovereign was to distribute the empire's new areas among his family members. He also sent a delegate to the Abbasid Caliph in Baghdad to state his acceptance of the authority of the Caliph and his aim to follow the way of Islam. In Tugrul Bey's time the borders of the Seljuk State expanded rapidly. In the one decade following the battle of Dandanaqan the borders of the State reached Herat, Sistan, Khwarezm, Kirman, and Amman. Making the dynasties in Persia dependent on him, Tugrul Bey took control of the city of Rey. He then moved the center of the Seljuk State to Rey.

Apart from the expansion of the Seljuk state's borders, one of Tugrul Bey's most important accomplishments was the series of raids he conducted on Anatolia with the help of the Turkmens. The Oghuzs began to immigrate in mass to the lands under Seljuk control. To establish order in these lands and to find a residence for the Turkmens who caused discomfort everywhere they entered, Tugrul Bey directed the Turkmens to Anatolia, which was then under Byzantine domination. In 1048 the Turkmens conducted several raids on Anatolia. During these raids, they defeated the Byzantines, the Armenians and the Georgians several times. Tugrul Bey even commanded one of these raids himself in 1054. After Tugrul Bey departed from Anatolia, the raids and conquests were continued by the princes, emirs and Turkmen Beys appointed by Tugrul Bey. Those raids and conquests prepared the ground for Anatolia's becoming the Turks' homeland.

Another important development in Tugrul Bey's time was the establishing of good relations with the Abbasid Caliph. Because of these relations the Seljuks' becoming an outstanding state in the Islamic world. Even at the beginning of his enthronement, Tugrul Bey had declared his dependency on the Caliph and had a *khutbe* read in his name. A kinship was established between the two parties with the Abbasid Caliph Kaim Biemrillah's marriage to Çağrı Bey's daughter. Apart from this, there was another reason behind the Seljuks' becoming a respected and outstanding country in the Islamic world. In those times the Abbasid was under the oppression of the Shiite Fatimids and the Buveyhogulları. Upon the Caliph's request for help to rid Baghdad of the Shiite oppressors in 1055, Tugrul Bey's forces entered the city and liberated it from the Buveyhogulları and the Fatimids. With this development the Seljuk State became the leader of the Islamic world and the protector of Sunnite Islam. After the Baghdad expedition, Tugrul Bey returned to Rey and died a year later in 1063. At the time of Tugrul Bey's death, the borders of the empire he had founded extended from the Amu Darya to the Euphrates Rivers.

Before his death Tugrul Bey appointed his nephew Suleyman as his successor. However, after Tugrul Bey's death, Suleyman was displaced in a power struggle with his brother, Alparslan. Alparslan ascended to power in 1064. Alparslan made some changes in the administration and appointed Nizamulmulk, the writer of *Siyasetnama*, as vizier. He made appointments to some high-ranking positions and set out for conquests. In the spring of 1064 Alparslan set out on the Azerbaijan expedition. He made the Armenians in Arran dependent on him. Ani (which was the center of the Bagrat Armenians and was famous for its rampart) and Kars were conquered. Ani was one of the most important Christian cities in the East. Its conquest thus caused a great deal of pleasure in the Islamic world. For these successes, Alparslan was given the title *Ebul Feth* (the Father of Conquest). In the subsequent year Alparslan set out on an expedition to the eastern region and moved towards Turkistan. He captured Cend after a series of conflicts. However, one of Alparslan's most important accomplishments - perhaps his most important accomplishment of all - was the defeat of the Byzantines in the Battle of Manzikert. This victory had great consequences both in the history of the Great Seljuk Empire and in Turkish history. The event that led to the Battle of Manzikert was Alparslan's entrance to Anatolia which was under the Byzantine domination at the time. Alparslan captured Georgia in the second Caucasian expedition. In 1069 he entered Anatolia and then planned to move towards Egypt to attack the Fatimi State. In 1070 he captured Manzikert, Ercis, Siverek, and Aleppo, and then planned to move towards Damascus. Upon hearing that the Byzantine emperor Romanos Diogenes had sent a great force to remove the Turki sh threat from the region, he changed his aim of heading towards Egypt and decided to stay in Anatolia to face the Byzantine forces.

## The Battle of Manzikert (August 26, 1071)

The Seljuk and Byzantine forces met in Manzikert on August 26, 1071. Alparslan won a great victory against the Byzantine forces. The Byzantine emperor Diogenes was taken captive. Diogenes was freed and sent home after a treaty was signed on September 3, 1071. According to this treaty, Byzantium would pay an annual tax to the Seljuk State and would supply military help to the Seljuks when asked. However, this treaty was not put into practice due to a change of power in the Byzantine Empire.

Perhaps the most important consequence of the Battle of Manzikert was its establishing a precedence for Turkish raids in Anatolia for the purpose of making it a permanent dwelling place. The process of Anatolia's becoming a Turkish homeland began with the victory at Manzikert. After this pivotal battle Alparslan gave his commanders the task of conquering all of Anatolia. Another significant consequence of the Battle of Manzikert was the reaction that it solicited in Europe. While the Turks' victory at Manzikert was met with enthusiasm in the Islamic world, in Christian Europe it aroused feelings of indignation and led to the preparations of the Crusades in order to rescue Byzantium from the Turks.

Sultan Alparslan died on November 24, 1072 as he proceeded towards Transoxiana to fight against the Kara-Khanid Khanate. He was followed by his son Melikshah, who he had chosen as his successor. Melikshah retained his father's vizier, Nizamulmulk. In the early period of his rule, Melikshah had to confront a rebellion organized by his uncle Kavurt. He also had to confront the Kara-Khanids' and Ghaznavids' violation of the

Seljuk borders. After he solved these problems, Melikshah sought to achieve further conquests. Anatolia was the territory that Melikshah most coveted. The conquest of Anatolia was hastened by the effective leadership of the Beys and other competent commanders. By 1075 all of Anatolia had passed into Turkish hands, with the exception of the western coastal regions. It was even possible to meet Turk men in such far off regions as Sapanca and Izmit (Nicomedia). By making use of power struggles inside the Byzantine Empire, Melikshah was also able to capture the city of Iznik (Niceae) and its surrounding territory. In Iznik he established the foundations of the Anatolian Seljuk Empire.

Fighting with Shiites also became one of the basic policies of the Seljuks. This policy was continued in Melikshah's time. As a result, the struggle with the Fatimid was continued. In 1072 Palestine and Jerusalem were captured. In 1076 Tripolidamascus and Syria were included in the Seljuk Empire. In 1085 the Mervani State situated around Diyarbakir was destroyed. In 1089 the Western and in 1090 the Eastern Kara-Khanid Khanates were destroyed and thus the borders of the State were expanded to the Great Wall of China. In 1092 Yemen and Aden were seized. In Mecca a *khutbe* was read in the name of Melikshah. Melikshah was given by the title "Ruler of the East and the West" by the Caliph. He was poisoned on November 20, 1092.

## Disintegration

Upon Melikshah's death there began what is known as the "hiatus period". The hiatus period was characterized by internal power struggles and stagnation. In this period, each of Melikshah's four sons held power: Mahmud (1092), Berkyaruk (1092-1104), Muhammed Tapar (1105-1118), and Sencer (1118-1156). Under the rule of Sencer, there began a period of recovery and reorganization in the Seljuk Empire. Sencer reasserted Seljuk power over the states that had broken away after his father's death. He renewed and reinforced Seljuk domination in Iraq, Azerbaijan, Iran, Transoxiana, and the Ghaznavid lands. In spite of these developments, the Seljuk Empire lost its previous power due to a series of negative developments. The Abbasid Caliphs began to struggle against the Seljuks to regain their previous political strength. In 1141 the Seljuk Empire was defeated by the Karahitay in the vicinity of Samarqand (this conflict is known as the Katvan War). In 1153 the Oghuzs rebelled against the Seljuk Empire over a tax dispute. The Oghuzs had previously been the Seljuk Empire's most arduous supporters. The Seljuk sultan fell captive to the Oghuzs during this rebellion. Three years later the sultan was freed and returned to power. The Seljuk Empire did not recover from these blows and came to an end in 1157 with the death of Sencer.

In accordance with the rules of the Turkish administrative system, the Great Seljuk State shared the existent and newly-conquered lands among the members of the dynasty. Consequently, as the central State continued its life, Seljuk states emerged that was dependent upon the central administration: Iraqi and Khorasan, Kirman, Syrian, and Anatolian Seljuks. When the central authority weakened after Melikshah's death, these Seljuk states gradually gained power. With the end of the Great Seljuk State they became independent structures.

The Iraqi and Khorasan Seljuks (1092-1194) were founded by Malikshah's grandson Mahmut. Mahmut had a power struggle with his uncle Sencer for some time, but Sencer won the struggle. When Sencer became the Seljuk Sultan, he left the western regions (the Iraq region) to his nephew. In this way the Iraqi Seljuks were formed. The Iraqi Seljuks were known for their struggle against the Abbasid caliphs who wanted to regain their lost political power. This state was removed from history by the Harzemshahs.

The Kirman Seljuks (1092-1187) were founded in Kirman (southern Iran) by Çağrı Bey's son Kavurd. Kavurd had struggled to come to power in the Great Seljuk State after Alparslan's death but died during that struggle. Kavurd's descendents kept Kirman dependent on the Great Seljuk State. The Kirman Seljuks were destroyed by the Oghuzs who had rebelled against the Great Seljuk State.

The Syrian Seljuks (1092-1117) were founded by Malikshah's brother Tutuş. Tutuş remained dependent on the Great Seljuk State until 1092. When Malikshah died, Tutuş declared his independence and established his own state. However, when Tutuş died in 1095, this state was divided into two branches, one being Aleppo and the other Damascus. As a result of the wars with the Crusaders, the two branches weakened. The Damascus branch collapsed in 1105 and the Aleppo branch in 1118.

The Anatolian Seljuks, or the Seljuks of Turkey, (1092-1277) will be handled in the section entitled "Anatolian Turkish States".

## The Khwarezmshahs (Harzemsahlar)

The basin where the Amu Darya River flows into the Aral Lake was called Khwarezm. The rulers of that region were called Khwarezmshahs. The founders of the Khwarezmshah State were the Khwarezm governors of the Great Seljuk State, Anushtegin's grandsons. The governors that came after Anushtegin tended to be independent. However, they could not find the opportunity to declare independence during the time that the Great Seljuk State was powerful. Upon Sencer's death in 1157, Il-Arslan declared the independence of the Khwarezmshahs. The capital of the state was the province of Gulgenç. The Khwarezmshah state developed and strengthened rapidly in the time of Il-Arslan. The borders of the state expanded towards Transoxiana, past eastern Turkistan, towards Iran and west of Azerbaijan. The State had its brightest period in the time of Alaaddin Muhammed. The Gurlus were taken under control and the Karahitays were defeated. Alladdin Muhammed was not successful however, against the Mongols. Not being able to stand against the Mongol attacks, the Khwarezmshah State began to collapse in 1220. Although the Khwarezmshah State recovered somewhat in the time of Celaleddin Khwarezmshah, its fall could not be prevented. After the fall of the state, the Khwarezm masses began to flee from the Mongol invasions by migrating to the west. Some of them went to Anatolia.

# CHAPTER 5

## Turkish States in Egypt and Syria

### 1. The Tolunogullari (868 - 905)

Egypt was conquered by Islamic armies in 639. Egypt then became one of the most important regions in the Islamic State. A governor and administrative offices for collecting taxes, collecting secret information and securing communication were appointed to Egypt by the Islamic State. This distribution of positions among different administrators was intended to protect the Islamic State's central authority by preventing a concentration of power in the hands of one local administrator. This system had weaknesses in solving some problems. It therefore became necessary to appoint powerful governors to the region. From time to time, governors who were originally Turkish were also appointed to the area.

One of these Turkish governors was Tolunoglu Ahmet. He was appointed to his father Bayik Bey's position as a governor by proxy. As soon as he came to Egypt, Ahmed discarded the Abbasid administrators. He made himself the sole authority in the region and then declared his independence. In a short while he constructed a strong fleet and army. Important developments in agriculture occurred in his time that significantly improved the economic condition of Egypt. Fustat (ancient Cairo), the capital of the state, became a wealthy center of culture. Tolunoglu constructed the Tolunoglu Mosque, which still exists today and is considered an important architectural work. He also constructed a hospital which has no equivalent in Egypt.

Tolunoglu Ahmed seized Syria in 878. The lands from the Euphrates to Maghreb were unified under his rule. He became ill when he went to Antioch to suppress a rebellion and died when he returned to Egypt. During his 16-year rule, Ahmed not only saved Egypt from the economic crisis it was undergoing, but also made Egypt a cultural center of attraction. After Ahmed, the state lost its former power. In 905 it was destroyed by the Abbasid State and re-connected to the Caliph authority.

The Tolunogullari had a great importance in Turkish Islamic history. The Tolunogullari family established the first Muslim Turkish dynasty in a region where a very small part of the population was Turkish. They administered the country well and founded a strong state.

## 2. The Ihshids (Akshids) (935 - 969)

About thirty years after the Tolunogullari Dynasty was destroyed, the Ihshid family founded a new dynasty in Egypt. The Ihshids were a military family from Fergana. The founder of the Ihshid Dynasty was Ebubekir Muhammed. His father Togaç, was one of the governors of Damascus in Tolunogullari's time. Muhammed was a governor who first worked in Syria and then in Egypt. He was appointed governor of Egypt in 935 and declared his independence by relying on the local Turkish population. At first he established good relations with the Abbasid Caliph, but later he cut off all ties with the Caliph.

As Muhammed's base of power became stronger, he endeavored to: a) protect Egypt from the Fatimid threat that emerged in the Near West, and b) take new territories under his control. He took Syria in 941, Mecca and Medina in 942, and then expanded his authority as far as Yemen.

Muhammed's time, like that of Tolunoglu Ahmed, was one of affluence. His descendents however, were not as successful. The Fatimids ended the Ihshid Dynasty in 969.

## 3. The Eyyubis (1171 - 1252)

The founder of the Eyyubis State was Selahaddin Eyyubi. He was a commander in Mosul Atabey Mahmud Zengi's army. In 1171 Selahaddin Eyyubi saved Egypt from the Fatimids who had overthrown the Ihshids. Removing the Fatimid Caliph, he made coins for the Abbasid Caliph and had *khutbe* read in his name. He served as governor under the authority of Nureddin Mahmud until Mahmud's death in 1174. In that year Selahaddin Eyyubi declared his independence and founded his own state. The administrating staffs of his state and most of the army were Turkish. The official language of the Eyyubi State was also Turkish. His policy was based on Sunni-Islam ideology, in this regard he followed the same political doctrine as the Seljuk State.

With his brother Turan Shah, Selahaddin conquered Syria and extended his dominion as far as Iraq. He became stronger as many Turkish clans in the Middle East joined his state. In 1187 Selahaddin defeated the Crusaders in the Hittin War and seized

Jerusalem and the coastal regions of Syria. After the Hittin War a third Crusade was organized, but the Crusaders were again unsuccessful against Selahaddin.

After Selahaddin's death a power struggle erupted among his family members for succession to the throne. During that struggle the Memluk commanders managed to take power. Turan Shah was the last Eyyubis sultan. He was displaced from power by Ayberg, one of the Memluk commanders. The Memluks were of Turkish origin.

## 4. The Memluks (The State of Turkey)

The Turkish Memluk State was founded in Egypt in the thirteenth century. Arabic writers of the time referred to this state as "Turkey". In contrast to other Turkish Islamic states, this state was not established by a dynasty. Memluk means "white slave," one who becomes a slave either by being captured during a war or by being sold. In Turkish Islamic history the term "memluk" came to refer to those people who worked under the command of a dynasty as salaried guardsmen with a distinguished position both in social and juridical terms. In the world of Islam, the Turkish Memluks were commonly used as military slaves from the Abbasid period onward. They became an important factor on which many Islamic states in the Middle East depended. The Memluk State was founded by the Memluks in the Eyyubi State. The founder of the state was Aybek et-Turkmani. Selahaddin Eyyubi, who came to power in 1159, continued the Abbasid tradition of forming an army from slaves. These slaves displayed great physical strength. They were either captured or bought in the northern Black Sea region by the Eyyubi army. Although there were some Circassians among them, most were Turkish. After Selahaddin Eyyubi, the Eyyubis took the tradition of employing slaves in the army a step further: they employed the most intelligent ones as high state offices.

These slave-soldiers were trained in two caserns. One casern was situated on Ravda Island in the Nile River near Cairo. In this casern there was Turk, mostly Kypchak soldiers who were called *Memalik-i Bahriye* (Naval Slaves). The other casern was again near Cairo and included Circassian soldiers who were called "Memalik-i Çerakise". The slave-soldiers who founded the Memluk State were from the Memalik-i Bahriye casern. In later years the soldiers of the Memalik-i Çerakise casern took control of the administration of the Memluk State.

These slave-soldiers became influential in the army and the state administration of the Eyyubi Dynasty and initiated a rebellion. The last Eyyubi sultan Turan Shah took harsh measures against the rebel slave-soldiers and slave-officers before being killed by them. The rebels then appointed Fiecer-Ud-Dur as the new sultan. Fiecer-Ud-Dur was the widowed wife of one of the older sultans, Malik Necmettin Salih. The rebels appointed Muizzüddin Ayberg as commander of the army. Fiecer-Ud-Dur eventually married Ayberg and handed the crown to him. The Memluk State founded by slave-soldiers and slave-officers lasted for more than 250 years. The years of Ayberg's rule were plagued by many internal conflicts. After Ayberg's death, his son Nurettin Ali assumed the reins of power. The Memluk administrative system however, was not dynastic and therefore did not recognize as legitimate the transference of authority from father to son. In 1259 Nurettin Ali was replaced by Seyfettin Kutuz.

In 1260, while the Memluks were resolving their internal conflicts, Mongol armies occupied Baghdad, killed the Caliph and began to approach the Egyptian border. The Memluk Sultan Kutuz sent an army commanded by Baybars to stand against the Mongol raiders. The two forces faced each other in the Ayn Calud region, where the Mongols were harshly defeated. The Memluks' victory at Ayn Calud prevented the Mongols from occupying Syria and Egypt. This also brought Syria and Egypt closer. The Turks fleeing from the Mongol invasion took refuge in the Memluk State and formed salaried military groups in the army.

After Kutuz, Baybars became the head of the Memluk State. Baybars understood that a great threat would be posed to the Memluk state if the Christians and the Mongols formed an alliance against it. This alliance would include the small Armenian Princedom in the North, the Franks on the coasts, the Cyprus Kingship, and the Ismails and Nuseyris in Syria and Egypt who opposed the Memluks Sunni policies. Baybars took tactful measures to prevent the formation of this Mongol-Christian alliance. Baybars established his own alliance with Golden Horn (the Altınordu State) against the Mongol Ilkhanate in Iran. He also formed an alliance with the Byzantines against the Crusaders in Syria. As Baybars re-established the Abbasid caliphate in Egypt, the Memluk State began to dominate the entire Islamic world. Baybars not only defended Syria against new attacks from the Ilkhanate, but he also eliminated the Ilkhanate presen ce in Syria. In 1277 he entered Anatolia and defeated the Mongols in Elbistan for the second time. Later he ended the Cilicia Armenian Princedom and ejected the Crusaders from Antioch.

Baybars' conquests strengthened the Memluk State. After his death his sons Berke and Sulemish came to the throne. They were soon deposed by Kalavun, who became the new ruler of the Memluk State. Kalavun's descandents ruled the Memluk State from 1279 to 1382. Berkuk ended the Kalavuns' dynasty in 1382 when he became the new ruler of the Memluks. Berkuk's displacement of the Kalavuns was made possible by the Circessian Memluks' seizure of power. This marked the beginning of a new era in the Memluk history.

Under Berkuk's leadership the Memluks established alliances with the Ottomans, the Golden Horn State, and the Principality of Kadi Burhanettin. These alliances were made to defend against the threat posed by Timur the Lame. After Berkuk's death in 1399 these alliances were broken off. The fifteenth century was not very generous to the Memluks. After a war fought between Berkuk's successor Ferec and Timur the Lame, the territory of Syria was lost. In addition to that, Egypt lost its former importance on the trans-continental trade route as the Portuguese began transporting Indian goods by way of the Cape of Good Hope. This resulted in the Memluk economy fell into a bad state.

The Memluks' relations with the Ottomans began to worsen in that period. The Memluks and the Ottomans competed for domination over the Turkmen principalities in southern Anatolia. The Memluks began taking sides in the struggles between the various Shahzades (princes) within the Ottoman Empire. These conflicts gave rise to a war between the Memluks and the Ottomans which lasted from 1485 to 1490. Neither side emerged victorious from the war. The Ottoman state however, was rapidly developing in contrast to the Memluk state. The Ottomans succeeded in conquering the Memluk State in 1517.

# CHAPTER 6

## The Anatolian (Turkish) Seljuk State

The Seljuk Sultans directed the Turks systematically to Anatolia. Although their founding of a state was not realized until the Battle of Manzikert in 1071, the Turks had started settling in the region much earlier.

The Turks' interest and settlement in Anatolia dates back to the pre-Islamic period. We have already stated that the Huns had conducted short-termed raids in Anatolia between 395 and 398. The most important Turkish raids in Anatolia however, were accomplished after the conversion to Islam. Kılıçarslan Bey, the father of the Seljuk Sultan Alparslan, had come to eastern Anatolia by way of Khorasan and Iran with a force of three thousand soldiers. The success of this expedition convinced the Seljuks that there was no force in the region that could stand against them. At this point the Seljuks began to consider Anatolia as an ideal place for establishing a homeland. During the reign of the first Seljuk emperor Tugrul Bey (1040-1063) they conducted frequent expeditions to Anatolia. Although there was no permanent Tu kish settlement in the region, the Turks had begun to struggle w.th Byzantium for Anatolian lands. The Seljuks' interest in Anatolia is evidenced in the relocation of their capital from Nishabur to Rey: Rey is further west than Nishabur and therefore closer to Anatolia. This profound interest led Tugrul Bey himself to come to Anatolia and take victorious command of the struggle against the Byzantines.

The Turks' advances in Anatolia from the time of Çağrı Bey's first expedition to the time Tugrul's death constitutes a series of great conquests. These came between the foundation of the Great Seljuk State and the Battle of Dandanaqan. During the rein of Tugrul Bey, the authority of the Byzantines was weakened in Anatolia. This created an ideal opportunity for preparing Anatolia as a homeland for the Turks. The Battle of Manzikert in 1071 that made it possible for the Turks to settle in Anatolia. Beginning in the twelfth century, during the reign of Alparslan, Anatolia took on the new name of "Turkey" (Turkiye). Having defeated the Byzantines in the Battle of Manzikert, the Turks realized that no force could resist them in the region. The Turks therefore began to conduct more raids into

Anatolia with the intention of making it their homeland. Alparslan charged his commanders and princes with the duty of conquering Anatolia. As the conquest of Anatolia (or Turkey) neared it completion, a new state emerged that was called the Anatolian Seljuk Turkish State.

After the Manzikert Victory in 1071, the Anatolian Seljuk State was not the only state founded in Anatolia. Such Turkmen Princes and Commanders as Artuk, Tutak, Danishmend, Saltuk, Mengucuk, Savtegin, and Afshin who fought with Alparslan against the Byzantines also conquered different Anatolian regions and founded their own principalities. Alparslan had given them the authority to establish new homelands in the territories they had seized.

The Anatolian Seljuk State emerged as a result of the intense migration of Turks to Anatolia after the Battle of Manzikert. The founder of the state was Kutalmışoğlu Suleyman Shah, who was the grandson of Arslan Yabghu, one of the four sons of Seljuk. Suleyman Shah was one of the Turkish commanders who took part in the conquests of Anatolia beginning in 1074. He was first active among the clans on the coast of Euphrates River and Urfa. He also besieged Antioch and Aleppo. However, after Suleyman Shah got into conflict with the Syria Seljuk ruler Atsiz, he turned his attention to the West.

During these times the Byzantine Empire was being shaken by inner conflicts and rebellions in the Balkans. Therefore Byzantium could not show any interest in the Turkish raids in Anatolia and the Turkish clans beginning to dwell there. Making use of that situation, Suleyman Shah entered central Anatolia and seized a fortress in the surroundings of Konya. After that, he took advantage of the struggle for power in the Byzantine administration and seized many cities and fortresses without difficulty. At last he conquered the great and historic Byzantine city of Iznik in 1078 and made it the capital of the state. Through these conquests, Suleyman Shah established the foundations of the Anatolian Seljuk State.

Suleyman Shah continued his conquests and expanded the borders of the state at Byzantium's expense. Having defeated the Byzantine army that came to Iznik to take the city back from the Turks, he proceeded on to Uskudar (known as "Chrysopolis" during the Byzantine era), a district of Istanbul. With the customhouse he founded there he began to collect customs from the ships passing through the Bosporus. When Alexis Comnenos came to power in Byzantium, the situation changed and the Turks began to withdraw. In a treaty signed in 1082, the Dragos Brook that lay in the Izmit Gulf was accepted as the border between the two states. Suleyman Shah's position was strengthened with that treaty.

After he signed the treaty with Byzantium, Suleyman Shah returned to Anatolia and in 1083 conquered Tarsus, Adana, and Missis. He also began to collect taxes from Malatya. Additionally, he came to Antioch by invitation of the Christians who were displeased with the Armenian Principality that had been founded there. With support from the Christians of Antioch, he seized the city. Those conquests were followed by the conquests of Antep and Iskenderun. Tutuş, the emir of Syria, was displeased with Suleyman Shah's conquests and the prestige that he had acquired. In a war that broke out between Suleyman Shah and Tutuş on June 5, 1086, Suleyman Shah was defeated and killed.

According the Suleyman Shah's wishes, Ebul Kasim assumed the reins of power in the Anatolian Seljuk State after his death. Ebul Kasim prevented the newly-founded state from disintegrating and conducted successful raids on Byzantium. At this time the Great Seljuk Sultan Malikshah sent out a large force to bring the Turkish Seljuks totally under his control. He was unsuccessful in this attempt due to his death. Malikshah's death also gave rise to another event: Kılıçarslan I, who was one of Suleyman Shah's sons and was then with Malikshah, returned from Khorasan to Iznik towards the end of 1092 and became the sultan of the Anatolian Seljuk State.

### Struggle for Unification between the Turks and the Crusaders

When Kılıçarslan I came to power he saw that the Anatolian Seljuk State lacked a strong central authority that was capable of unifying the region. Turkish commanders in various parts of Anatolia had formed their own principalities. The Byzantines were also on the attack, against both the Turks and the Crusaders. Kılıçarslan I also thought that his father-in-law, Çaka Bey, posed a great threat to the Anatolian Turks. Çaka Bey had already founded a state in Izmir, formed his own fleet, and taken control of the neighboring islands and the Dardanelles.

Kılıçarslan I began to take action. First he signed a contract with Byzantium against Çaka Bey and deposed him 1094. Having eliminated his threats from the West, Kılıçarslan I then directed his attention to the East. In 1096 he besieged Malatya which was in the hands of the Armenians. During the siege of Malatya, Kılıçarslan I learned that the first Crusaders were arriving in Anatolia. He immediately ended the seige and returned to the capital. The Crusaders were defeated by the Seljuk army led by Kılıçarslan I's brother Davud. When Kılıçarslan I reached Iznik however, the second wave of Crusaders had already besieged the city. Kılıçarslan I could not enter Iznik. Since the siege lasted a long time, Iznik was left to the Byzantines with a contract signed in 1097. Kılıçarslan I then moved the capital to Konya. With the military support of the Danishmend Dynasty, Kılıçarslan I fought against the Crusaders in the surroundings of Eskisehir. He was successful in that fight but he could not stop the Crusaders. Given this result, he decided to fight against the Crusaders not by doing pitched battle with them, but by following the policy of weakening the enemy. Having fought against them until 1102, Kılıçarslan I destroyed the Crusaders totally on that date and thus removed the threat that they posed.

After the First Crusade was finished, the Turks began a process of socio-political reconstruction. Iznik had passed into the hands of the Byzantines and Konya had become the new capital. Now there was a new effort to make Anatolia a secure place again. Kılıçarslan I struggled with the other Turkish principalities to establish unity in the region and to expand his state. In this expansion process the Anatolian Seljuk State became a neighbor to the area dominated by the Great Seljuk State. Kılıçarslan I had also seized Mosul in the expansion process and this event was disapproved of by the Great Seljuk State. The regional disagreement quickly turned into a conflict between the two states. At the end of the war between the Great Seljuk Emir Çavli and Kılıçarslan (which took place on the side of the Habur River in 1107) Kılıçarslan I was defeated and killed.

Like the death of Suleyman Shah, the death of Kılıçarslan I created an administrative problem in the state. Making use of this situation, Byzantium fought the Turks back into central Anatolia. At first Kılıçarslan I's son Shehin Shah came to power. Shehin Shah was displaced by his brother Mesud with the help of the Danishmend Dynasty. Mesud entered Konya in 1116 and took his place on the throne. In his rule of about forty years, Mesud first saved the Anatolian Seljuk State from disappearance and then made it the most important power in Anatolia.

The first years of Mesud's governance passed under the patronage of Emir Gazi, the leader of the Danishmend Dynasty that had become the most powerful country in the region. Emir Gazi was also Mesud's father-in-law. That situation continued until Emir Gazi died in 1134. Having the opportunity to act independently after that date, Mesud took back Ankara, Çankırı ("Changra" in ancient times), and Kastamonu from the Danishmends. In 1144 he seized Elbistan and moved towards Maraş, which was in the hands of the Crusaders. When he heard that the Byzantine Emperor Manuel Comnenos was moving towards Konya, he returned to the capital and resoundingly defeated the Byzantine forces.

While Mesud was strengthening his forces, the second Crusaders led by the German king Konrad III and the Frankish king St. Louise had reached Anatolia. Mesud defeated the German army in 1147 in the surroundings of Eskisehir. St. Louise then gave up entering Anatolia. Instead, St. Louise went to Antalya through the coast and from there he proceeded to Akka by sea. Mesud then waged harsh attacks on the Cilicia Armenians. He made the Danishmends dependent on him. Mesud died in 1155, after having made the Anatolian Seljuk State the most powerful state in the region.

Before his death, Mesud partitioned his country between his sons. According to this partition, Kılıçarslan II would stay in Konya and his brothers would be dependent on him. The brothers did not accept this arrangement and began to struggle with Kılıçarslan II for power. Kılıçarslan II dealt with his brothers and with external forces that tried to make use of the situation, including: the Byzantine Emperor Manuel Comnenos, the Cilicia Armenian Princedom, Musul, and Aleppo, Atabeg, Nureddin Zengi, and the Danishmend Bey Yaghibasan. Kılıçarslan II first of all won the struggle with his brothers and established internal order in the Anatolian Seljuk State. Then he secured the western borders of the state by signing a pact of non-aggression with the Byzantines in 1162 and directed his attention to the East. In 1163 he made the Danishmend Dynasty ineffective and took back the place s seized by Nureddin Zengi. He also solved the problems with the other principalities.

## The Battle of Myriokephalon (1176)

The successes of Kılıçarslan II had begun to displease Byzantium. As everything was going well for the Turks in the east, began to intensify their raids on the Byzantine regions in the west. To confront this problem, the Byzantine emperor Manuel Comnenos formed a great army against the Turks and rejected all the offers of peace made by Kılıçarslan II. The Byzantine army, which was reinforced with Frank, Hungarian, Serbian, and Pecheneg soldiers, left Istanbul in the spring of 1176. On September 1, 1176, it was badly defeated by the Turkish army led by Kılıçarslan II in the Myriokephalon Vale near Denizli. Comnenos was set free with the condition of removing his fortifications in Anatolia and paying massive amends. This victory ended the Byzantines' hopes of taking Anatolia back from the Turks after the Battle of Manzikert. It proved that Anatolia was not under a Turkish invasion as the Christians had claimed, but was instead the Turks' true homeland. After the Battle of Myriokephalon, Byzantium would not dare to arrange further assaults on the Turks.

After he solved the Byzantine problem, Kılıçarslan II brought an end to the Danishmend Dynasty and thus removed his adversary in the east. The Turkmen forces destroyed the Armenian Cilicia Princedom and seized its lands. They also seized Silifke and expanded their holdings into Syria and Al Jazeera. The Seljuks' western border reached as far Denizli.

## Sharing the Country among the Princes and Afterwards

After a long life of governance and struggle, Kılıçarslan II became old and tired. He thus divided the country between his eleven sons in 1186. He himself stayed in Konya and administered the country via his vizier. This situation soon gave rise to a struggle for the throne among his sons. To the disorder which emerged as a result of the struggle for the throne was the added threat of the Third Crusade. In 1187 upon Salahaddin Eyyubi's seizing Jerusalem, the Christians had decided to organize a new Crusade. Although Kılıçarslan II tried to be cautious and sought a ground for agreement with the Crusaders, his sons behaved differently. The Crusaders entered Konya and ruined the city. After this catastrophe, Kılıçarslan took refuge with his son Giyaseddin Keyhusrev, with whom he remained until his death in 1192. After Kılıçarslan II's death, Giyaseddin Keyhusrev ascended to power. His brothers however, did not accept his enthronement. Whoever came to the throne in this period was bound to experience difficulties, and this would be the main weakness of the state. Giyaseddin Keyhusrev would also not remain in power for long. In 1196 his brother Ruknuddin Suleyman Shah started to move his forces towards Konya. Giyaseddin, not wanting to take the risk of fighting with his brother, took refuge in Byzantium. As a consequence, Ruknuddin Shah came to power in the Anatolian Seljuk State.

Suleyman Shah had made a great effort to re-establish unity among the Turks. He defeated the Armenian King Leon and the Byzantine Empire. He even made the Byzantines pay taxes. He seized some lands from the Mengudjeks and the Artuqids. In 1201 he ended the Saltuk principality, which was another Turkish principality in Anatolia. When Suleyman Shah died in 1207, since his son Kılıçarslan III was very young, the Turkmen commanders invited Giyaseddin Keyhusrev from Byzantium to Konya. Giyaseddin's second rule was quite successful. The Trebizond Rum Empire was defeated and the Black Sea trading road was taken under control. With the conquest of Antalya in 1207, the Turks gained access to a sea route. The Armenian Kingship was defeated, and the Eyyubis were prevented from seizing Syria and Anatolia. Giyaseddin died in 1211.

## The Brightest Time of the Anatolian Seljuks

After Giyaseddin's death, Izzeddin Keykavus came to occupy the Seljuk throne (1211-1220). He was followed by Alaaddin Keykubat. With a fleet formed in 1226 in Sinop, Alaaddin Keykubat set off to conquer Sagduk, which was an important trading port in Crimea. After the conquest of Sagduk, many Russian principalities and Kypchaks commanders were taken under control. The land forces of the state seized all the coastal regions as far as Silifke. Another development in the naval field was the seizing of an important center in the Mediterranean Sea. Keykubat besieged today's Alanya fortress both from the land and the sea and took possession of it in 1233. The city and the tower were re-constructed and re-named "Alaiye" in dedication to the Sultan. The first naval docks of the Anatolian Seljuk State were established there by Keykubat. Alaiye became a center in which the sultans passed their winters.

While Alaaddin was dealing with problems inside Anatolia,

the Mongol threat that had emerged in the heart of Asia was rapidly spreading towards the West. Celaleddin, the leader of Khwarezmshah, ran away from the Mongols in 1225 and went to Azerbaijan. Celaleddin's relationship with Alaaddin was good in the beginning. Yet when Celaleddin harshly destroyed Ahlat, which belonged to the Seljuks, the two leaders fell into conflict. Keykubat got the support of his Eyyubian allies and fought with Celaleddin. Although they should have united against their common enemy, the two armies faced each other on August 10, 1230, in Yassi Cemen near Erzincan. Khwarezm's forces were badly defeated. By this time the Mongol threat had reached the gates of Anatolia. Keykubad had already become aware of the threat that the Mongols posed. In order to defend his country from invasion he accepted the heavy demands that the Mongols raised. Yet he still took the required precautions. He strengthened the towers in the state's border cities and he began to seek alliances. Keykubat died in 1237 before he could complete these projects. His time was the brightest era of the Anatolian Seljuks in military, political, and economic terms. The expeditions he arranged made the trading roads secure. The caravanserais he built and his trade policy produced economic development. He also made efforts to develop science and culture in the country. Due to his successful governance, the Abbasid Caliph gave him the title "Great Sultan."

## The Decline

After Keykubat, the leading personalities of the state brought Giyaseddin Keyhusrev II to power. That ruler lacked his father's administrative and military abilities. In the first years of his rule he remained under the influence of his commander Saadettin. Kopek made him discard all the eminent statesmen who could be his adversaries. It continued this way until 1239. At that time Kopek was hanged and intelligent statesmen began to be effective again in the governance of the country. Although there had been some recovery in the state, it did not become possible to remove the political and religious weaknesses of the state. The Baba Ishak Rebellion, which emerged with religious and economic objectives, was hardly quenched. This rebellion showed that the state was so weakened that it could hardly quench a rebellion or solve its inner problems.

In the end the Mongols entered Anatolia with a great force and fought with the Anatolian Seljuk army in 1243 in Kosedag, near Sivas. In July of 1243, the Seljuk army experienced a crushing defeat. The Mongols governed Anatolia for over half a century. The Seljuk Sultans that came after Giyaseddin Keyhusrev II governed like puppets in the hands of the Mongols. Eventually, the Anatolian Seljuk State totally disappeared in 1308.

After the Kosedag war in 1243, the Anatolian Seljuk State entered a period of rapid collapse. The sultans that came to power before the collapse of the state in 1308 governed as dependents of the Mongols. That is to say, the governance of the country passed to the Mongols. This administrative situation also brought about an economic collapse, and it raised the possibility of the Anatolian Seljuk state totally disappearing. The Turkmen commanders that wanted to make use of this situation, upon the Mongols' beginning to weaken in the region, separated from the Anatolian Seljuk State and founded their own principalities, such as Eretna, Karamans, Germiyans, Aydins, Hamids, Karasi, Dulkadir and Ramazan. This marked the beginning of a second "Principality Period". These principalities, which especially struggled with the Byzantines, played an important role in the Islamization of Anatolia and in its becoming Turkish.

# CHAPTER 7

## Turkish States in India

### 1. The Delhi Turkish Sultanate

Islam came to India in the time of the Umayyads, but its acceptance on a massive level occurred in the time of the Turkish Ghaznavid state. After the destruction of the Ghaznavids, the Ghoris (Gurlular) began to dominate. After the Ghoris different dynasties were founded and ruled in the region. The Turkish domination continued there with the Qutbis, the Shemsis, the Balabans, and the Halacs (Kalacs) from 1206 to 1414.

Muizuddin Muhammed, the ruler of the Ghoris who came to power in 1203, charged the Turkish commander Aybak with the conquest of India. Aybak increased his importance during these conquests. He had mosques and medresa (theological schools) built in the places he conquered. He made peace, tranquility and justice prevail in those places. Upon Muizuddin Muhammed's death in 1206, Aybak seized Delhi, declared his independence and founded his own state. Though he occupied Ghazna for a time, he could not keep it under control for long. He seized all of northern India from Peshaver to the Tibet Mountains. When Aybak died in 1210, Aram Shah became the Sultan. In 1211 Shemseddin Iltutmush, who was Aybak's son-in-law and one of his commanders, overthrew Aram from power and declared himself the Sultan.

Iltutmush, the founder of the Shemsi Dynasty which continued to exist until 1266, first took under his authority those commanders who had declared independence after Aybak's death. Afterwards, he made successful conquests and expanded his area of dominion. He included Punjap, Lahor, and Multan into his domain. Accepting the Turkish masses fleeing from the Mongol invasion, he helped Turkish culture develop in northern India. He was the first Delhi Sultan accepted by the Abbasid Caliph. After Iltutmush's death in 1236, his daughter ruled the country for a while. Shortly thereafter the commanders rebelled and engaged in a struggle for the throne that produced chaos in the country. In that process, the Mongols entered Sind, Multan, and Punjap. In 1241 they ruined Lahor. Balaban, one of

Iltutmush's commanders, constructed a great force and successfully withstood against the Mongol attacks in 1258 and 1259. He re-seized the throne from the Mongols and became the Sultan with the name 'Giyaseddin.'

Establishing a new dynasty with the name Giyaseddin, Balaban strengthened his authority by getting the support of the Turks who took refuge in India as a result of the Mongol invasion. He bloodily quenched rebellions that emerged against his authority. He strongly established Turkish dominance in India until 1287. However, since Giyaseddin had not provided a good successor before dying, the sultans who came after his death remained under the influence and authority of their commanders. In 1290, three years after Giyaseddin's death, the chief of the Halac Turks (Firuz Shah) ended the Balaban Dynasty and became the New Delhi Sultan with the nickname 'Celaleddin.'

Celaleddin Firuz Shah successfully prevented Mongol attempts at invasion between 1291 and 1292 and captured most of the Mongols. Those who were Muslim among the captive Mongols were re-located near Delhi and began to serve the Delhi Turkish Sultanate. When Celaleddin died in 1296, Alaaddin Muhammed Shah became his successor. Alaaddin Muhammed Shah, who became one of the most important rulers of the Halac, made his country affluent through economic and administrative reforms. Fighting off the Mongols and the Hindus, he expanded the borders of the state. He took under his control almost all of northern India and enlarged the borders of the state to the coastal regions in southern India. After his death in 1316, his son Mübarek Khan became his successor. Mübarek Khan's rule was not as successful as that of his father's. When he used the same violence that he had used to quench rebellions on his inner circle, a great sense of discomfort arose against him. He was assassinated in 1320. After his death, the commander of the front regions, Melik Tugluk, ended the Halac Dynasty and began the era of the Tugluklar Dynasty by becoming the new Sultan of Delhi.

Soon after he came to power, Gazi Melik Tugluk established tranquility and peace in the state and began conquering new lands. He Seized Varandal and Birdar. When Melik Tugluk died in 1325, his son Muhammed Tuluk Shah became his successor. To keep the lands seized in the time of Muhammed under control, Devletabad was established as a new administrative center. Muhammed died in 1351. After that, a great chaos emerged in the country. The commanders declared independence and as a consequence five different states emerged. When Firuz Shah came to power, he recovered the state and established unity. He put into use many administrative, financial and economic reforms. He re-arranged the tax system. He gained the appreciation of all the Muslim and non-Muslim groups under his rule with his fair administration. However, when he died in 1388, chaos returned to the country and there began struggles for the throne between the shahzades. This situation continued until at last Timur Khan seized the lands of the Delhi Sultanate. Afterwards, the Afghan Seyidis ended the Tugluk Dynasty.

## 2. The Babur Empire (1526 - 1858)

Towards the end of the sixteenth century, apart from the Ottoman State, two states had decisive roles in the politics of the Islamic world: the Babur Empire and the Safavids.

The Babur Empire was founded in 1526 in India by Babur, who was the grand grandson of the Chagatai Turk, Timur Khan. Babur, who was the son of the Fergana dynast Omer Shah Mirza, came to power instead of his father. During the struggle between the Safavids and Uzbeks that took place in the region in the beginning of the sixteenth century, he settled in Samarqand with the support of the Safavids. When the Uzbeks defeated the Safavids in 1512, he had to withdraw to Kabul. Thinking that he would not be able to survive in Central Asia, he turned to India. In 1526, after having won the Battle of Panipat, he went to the Lodi Sultanate and founded a state in India. The capital of the state was Agra. When Babur Shah died in 1530, the borders of his state extended from the Vindiya Mountains in the south to Amu Darya River in the north. After his death, his son Humayun became his successor.

Humayun spent the first years of his rule establishing order and unity in the country. In this period the Afghan Shirshah, who became the greatest enemy of the Baburs, badly defeated Humayun and forced him to withdraw to Lahor. Humayun had to leave Agra and took refuge in the Safavid Dynasty. The governance of India passed to the Suris (Pashtuns). Humayun, who remained with the Safavids by that time, took the support of the Safavids and seized Afghanistan, Punjap and its surrounding regions. He then defeated the Suris in the Battle of Machivera in 1555 and again had the opportunity of ruling India. This victory is accepted as the second foundation date of the Babur Empire.

In the place of Humayun, who died in 1556, came his son Akbar Shah.

Akbar Shah was one of the most important rulers of the Baburs. He seized such places as Bengal, Kabul, and Kashmir, and expanded the borders of the state. He made renovations in the fields of economics and administration. He established good relations with the Ottomans, Safavids, and Uzbeks, and followed a policy of peace instead of war. He proposed that the Ottomans follow a common policy against the Portuguese who were active in the Indian Ocean, but he was not successful in that attempt due to the distance between the two states. Cihangir, who came to power in 1603 after Akbar, quenched the Afghan rebellions in Bengal. During Cihangir's rule, the Netherlands, Portugal, France, and England began to follow a colonialist policy in India. Cihangir gave the Europeans permission to construct trade foundations there. He thus prepared the ground for the later English domination of India. When Cihangir died in 1627, his son Shah Cihan came to power.

Shah Cihan took control of all the Muslim states existing in India and thus established unity. He also built good relationships with the Ottomans, Safavids, and Europeans. However, in 1632 when the Portuguese colonists in Hugli began to seek slaves in Bengal, he intervened and forced them to stay only in one city and not meddle with cities under others' rule. Shah Cihan became ill and died in 1652. After his death, fights began for power among his sons. Defeating his brothers, Evrengzib Alemgir declared himself the Sultan in Agra in 1658.

The period when Evrengzip ruled became the brightest period of the Baburs. The friendship with the Safavids was continued. Delegates of friendship were sent to Mecca and great financial support was presented there. In the time of Sultan Suleyman II, the Ottomans sent a delegate to the Babur Empire. Thus the friendship with the Ottomans was developed. To balance the population of the Muslims with that of the Hindus, a great Muslim population was transferred to the region from Turkistan, located in the big cities, and enlisted in the army. Evrengzip became ill and died in 1707.

After Evengzip, the state weakened and the rulers that came to power after him were especially ineffective against external threats and intrusions. Meanwhile Nadir Shah Afshar, who had destroyed the Safavids in Persia and founded his own dynasty there, arranged an expedition to India in 1738. First he invaded

Kabul and then Punjcap and Delhi. At the end of the expedition he took the Hint treasures to Persia. The Europeans also took advantage of the situation of the Baburs. Shah Alem, who came to power in 1760, was the first Babur sultan who accepted the dominion of the English. In his time, the English made their dominion in India more permanent and expanded their area of influence. In time, the names of the Babur rulers were removed from the coins and reading khutbe in the name of these rulers was prohibited.

The last Babur emperor, Bahadir Shah, began a great rebellion against the English in 1857. He had coins made for him and khutbe read in his name. The English harshly quenched the rebellion. 30,000 people were killed in Delhi. Bahadir Shah was captured and died in 1862 in the hands of the English. The Babur Empire ended with Bahadir Shah's imprisonment. Afterwards, the English made India a colony and began to administer it from London in 1858.

# CHAPTER 8

## The Turkish Khanates in the Northern Black Sea Region

### 1. The Golden Horde (Altınordu) State

The Golden Horde State was founded in 1241 by Genghis Khan's grandson Batu Khan on land extending from the Black Sea to Hungary. Its capital city was Sarai or Saray, one of the largest cities of the medieval world. Batu Khan seized the Lower and Central Volga regions, the Caucasian lands in between Khwarezm and Azerbaijan, and the Kypchaks steppe. In 1257, Batu's brother Berke became the sultan. Berke was the first Mongol ruler who accepted Islam. Having established an alliance with Baybars, the Sultan of Egypt, he attacked Hulagu, the ruler of Persia, Iraq, and Anatolia, and destroyed his administration in 1262.

In Berke Khan's time, Islam spread rapidly among the Mongols who came to the northern regions of the Black Sea. The Mongols under the rule of the Altınordu State in the Kypchaks and Kuman Turk regions became influenced by Turkish culture after they became Muslim. They forgot their mother tongues and became Turkish. After Berke Khan, Muslim rulers came to power. Uzbek Khan (1313-1341) and all the rulers that came after him were Muslim. Uzbek Khan made Islam the official religion of the state. He made Sarayberke the capital city. After the death of Canibek Khan in 1359, inner conflicts began in the Golden Horde State which resulted in its weakening. The Russians made use of this situation and defeated the Golden Horde army in 1380. The unity and recovery in the state achieved by Toktamış Khan, who came to power later, continued until Timur's military expeditions against the Golden Horde began in 1395. In 1398, Toktamış Khan had to take refuge with the Prince of Lithuania. After that, the state disintegrated into such states as the Great Golden Horde (1432-1502), the Astrakhan Khanate (1466-1557), the Khanate of Kazan (1445-1552), the Crimean Khanate (1430-1783) and the Uzbek Khanate.

## 2. The Khanate of Kazan

The Kazan Khanate was founded in 1437 in the region where the Volga Bulgarians lived by Ulug Muhammed Khan, one of the old Khans of the Golden Horde. Its population consisted of settled and nomadic Turks and Finns. Ulug Muhammed Khan (1437-1445) struggled with the Principalities of Moscow. Having been defeated, the Russians accepted Ulug Muhammed Khan's domination. The Russians agreed to pay an annual tax, to let the Kazan officers work in Russian cities, and they gave the region on the side of Oka River to Shahzade Kasim as a homeland. Via the Kasim Khanate founded on the side of Oka River, the Moscow Kniaz was taken under control.

In a period when struggle for the throne became more tense, Ivan III of the Moscow Principality married Sofia from the Byzantine royal family and declared his independence from Turkish domination in 1480. The Russians entered Kazan in the summer of 1487. Although the Kazan Khan Muhammed Emin (1502-1518) fought off the Russians from Kazan in 1506, he could not totally remove the threat posed by them. Kazan began the dominion of the Crimean Khanate in 1521, and of the Astrakhan Khanate in 1552. Throughout this period it faced constant Russian attacks. Ivan the Terrible, with the support of Europe, entered Kazan in the beginning of August 1552. After a terrible fight between the two forces, the Russians entered Kazan and captuared Muhammed Khan and his circle. Cultural and historical constructions and important places were ruined during the invasion. The treasures of the city and the state were wrecked by the Russians. In the end, Russian dominion was established in Kazan. The rebellions for independence that arose later were bloodily quenched. The surviving Kazan Turks are now known as the Tatars.

## 3. The Crimean Khanate

The founder of the Crimean Khanate was Batu Khan's brother, Haci Giray. The Golden Horde Khanate and its ruler Toktamış were badly shaken by their defeat at the hands of Timur in 1391 - 1395. After this defeat the commanders in the Crimea began to fight for independence. Haci Giray, who was one of those commanders, declared independence in 1441 and founded the Crimean Khanate. In the time that he was the khan, Haci Giray took control of the Taman Kabartay and Kypchak regions. He established an alliance with the Moscow Principality against the Golden Horde and with the Ottomans against the Genovese. The struggle for power that arose after his death made the country vulnerable to external attacks. In that process, the Crimean administrators asked for help from the Ottoman State against the Golden Horde and the Genovese. Upon that, with a great fleet he sent to the region, Mehmed II seized the Genovese colonies on the coastal parts of Crimea and took the Crimean Khanate under the protection of the Ottoman Empire (1475). Via the protection of the Ottomans, the Crimeans kept the Russians away from their lands for a long time.

After the Ottoman Empire began to weaken in the seventeenth century, the Russians (who wanted to extend their area of domination to the Black Sea) began increasing their attempts to invade Crimea. In 1736, the Crimean peninsula was invaded for the first time. The Ottoman-Russian War that took place between 1768 and 1774 brought the Crimean Khanate to an end. In the Treaty of Kucuk Kayanarca (Kuchuk Kainarji), which was signed as a result of the defeat of the Ottomans in the war, the Ottoman State had to accept the independence of Crimea. Crimea however, could not guard its independence. In 1783 the Russians seized Crimea.

## 4. The Astrakhan Khanate

The Astrakhan Khanate was founded in 1466 by Kasim Khan, who was a descendent of the Golden Horde Khan Muhammed. The Astrakhan Khanate was founded in the city of Astrakhan (Ejderhan, Astragan) and its surroundings, on the region where the Itil (Volga) River flows into the Caspian Sea. Astrakhan, which was the capital city of the khanate, was on an important trading route. It became rich due to contact with wealthy countries and nomadic tribes that traded in the city. The central authority began to weaken in time as the city was constantly confronted with foreign attacks. Besides, the facts that the population was nomadic and that the local chieftains gained power during the foreign intrusions also played an important role in the weakening of the central authority. In this regard, permanence and firmness could not be achieved and thus the khanate could not last long.

Since the times of Kasim Khan (1466-1490) and his brother Abdulkerim Khan (1490-1504) alliances were established with the Golden Horde and Russia. This created a peaceful atmosphere. When the Golden Horde State collapsed in 1502, the Crimean Khanate and Nogays attempted to seize Astrakhan. As a result, the Khanate was worn by struggles with those states that continued until 1525, and also by the constant change of khans. Although Huseyin Khan signed a contract with the Crimean Khanate in 1523, the khanate was exposed to pressure by the Russians who wanted to expand their lands to the east. The Crimean Khan, Shahin Bey, entered Astrakhan in 1549. He ruined the city and captured most of its population, together with Yagmurcu Khan. Yagmurcu Khan was able to get free from imprisonment and returned to throne with the intervention of the Ottomans.

The struggle between the Crimean, Kazan and Astrakhan khanates served the interests of the Russians. Making use of this situation, the Russians removed the Kazan Khanate in 1552. With a sudden attack the Russians seized Astrakhan in 1556 and ended to the Astrakhan Khanate.

## 5. The Kasim Khanate (1445-1681)

The Kasim Khanate was founded in 1445 by Kasim, the Kazan Khan Ulug Muhammed's son. The Kasim Khanate was located in the city of Gorodets (Kasim) that was situated on the side of the Oka River to keep Moscow under control. However, the khanate became a dominion of the Moscow Principalities in a short while and was used by them as a means of keeping the Turks under control. The administrators of the khanate, who were controlled by Russian governors, remained in their positions until 1681.

## 6. The Khanate of Sibir

The Khanate of Sibir was one of the khanates that emerged as a result of the disintegration of the Golden Horde. The founder of the khanate was Taybuga. Its capital was the city of Sibir, near today's Tumen, and it was founded on land extending north of today's Mongolia going towards Siberia.

With the rule of Sibir Khan (1563-1598), the state began to be called by his name. Sibir Khan fought off the Russians from Siberia in 1584. However, the strong Russian forces re-entered Siberia after a short while. After Sibir Khan's death in 1598, seeing that the main obstacle that prevented them from seizing Siberia no longer existed, the Russians invaded all of Siberia until 1683.

## 7. The Nogai Khanate

Nogai, who was one of the important commanders of the Golden Horde State, behaved with partial independence as he served for the Golden Horde. Upon the disintegration of the Golden Horde, he founded the Nogai Khanate with the tribes under his authority. The capital city of the Nogai Khanate was Saraycik, which was in the region where the Yayik River flowed into the Caspian Sea. The population of the khanate mostly consisted of Kypchak Turks. The Khanate was influential in the territories of today's Kazakhstan. The Khanate was divided into a few branches after it was destroyed by the Kazans and the Astrakhans. Some of these branches formed the Great Nogai Horde and accepted Russian domination. Those that did not accept Russian domination continued their existence in various parts of northern Caucasia.

In the end, Russia seized the whole of Siberia by 1604. It first extended its sovereignty over Kyrgyzs who were living in Upper Yenisei River, then in the Crimea in 1783, in northern Caucasia in 1859, in Tashkent (the capital city of Uzbekistan) in 1865, and in Bkuhara Khanate in 1868. Lastly, by taking Turkmenistan under its control in 1884, all Turkish countries or regions in Siberia, the northern Black Sea, northern Caucasia and Central Asia except Eastern Uyghurs were brought under Russian rule.

# CHAPTER 9

## Turkish States Founded in Anatolia and Persia

### 1. The Timurid Dynasty

The Timurid dynasty was founded by Timur Khan who was originally Mongol but well trained in Turkish culture. In the second half of the fourteenth century there was chaos in the Chagatai Khanate of Turkistan. The authority of the khans who were descendents of Genghis Khan was shaken and the administration passed into the hands of tribal chiefs. Timur, who was a member of the Barulas tribe, formed a dominion in Transoxiana in 1370 and came to power in Samarqand.

Timur Khan was one of the greatest military geniuses ever recorded in history. He arranged many expeditions to expand the territories of his state. First, in the expeditions he arranged in 1371 and 1379 he connected Khwarezm to his dynasty. He made five expeditions against the Uyghurs until he took them under his control. He supported Toktamış Khan during the power struggle in the Golden Horde State and helped him sit on the throne. However, when Toktamış got stronger, he began to see him as his adversary and the two began to fight. Defeating Toktamış three times, he made the Golden Horde State dependent on him. Afterwards, he proceeded as far as the Ukraine and took the Genovese and Venetian colonies in Crimea and the surrounding areas. He also defeated the Christian groups and unified the Slavic princes in northern Caucasia, and seized northern India and Delhi in 1399.

In 1399, after Timur had won all the wars he had fought, he set out on an expedition that continued for seven years. He made the Georgian Kingship obey his rule. The Kara Koyunlu (Qara Qoyunlu or Black Sheep Turkmen) ruler Kara Yusuf deserted Iraq after Timur entered the region. Timur seized Sivas, Malatya, and Besni and then moved towards Syria. He took Antep, Aleppo, Hama, Humus, and Damascus under his authority. The governance of Syria and Lebanon passed from the Memluks to his hands.

Timur's growing strength made him the main adversary of the Ottomans in the region. When the Principality previously seized by Bayezid I passed into Timur's hands and the commanders fleeing from Timur took refuge in the Ottoman State were added, a war between the two forces became unavoidable. The Ankara War between the two forces ended with Timur's victory but the consequences of this victory would give rise to many negative situations for Turkish history in the coming years. After the Ankara War, Timur occupied the Ottoman capital of Bursa and confiscated the treasures of the Ottoman State. He re-distributed to the commanders of Anatolia their lands on the condition that they would remain faithful to him. In this regard, Turkish unity in Anatolia was spoiled. He also forced the Byzantines to pay taxes. Thus, Timur had made the Ottoman, Memluk, Byzantine, Trebizond Rum, Golden Horde and India states dependent on his empire. In th e lands he seized he replaced the Genghis law that had been applied for a long time with that of Islam. Afterwards, he began his expedition to the East. Timur died during that expedition in 1405, as he was moving towards China.

The empire was shared between Timur's sons and grandsons. The state lost its former power. In 1420 his son Shahruh became the sole ruler of the empire after a fifteen-year struggle with his brothers and nephews. The struggle for the throne began again however, after Shahruh's death. Ulug Bey became the victor during that struggle and sat on the Timurid throne. Before coming to power, Ulug Bey was an astronomer and mathematician who dedicated himself to research in libraries and observatories. He was a sage and thus was detached from politics. In 1449 he was killed by his son who was provoked by his political adversaries. Struggles for the throne began again until the Timurid Dynasty, which was weakened with inner conflicts, was destroyed by the Uzbeks in 1507.

## 2. The Ak Koyunlu (Aq Qoyunlu) Dynasty

The Ak Koyunlu Dynasty ruled in the fifteenth century in eastern Anatolia, Azerbaijan, and Iraq. The founders of the dynasty belonged to the Bayindir tribe of the Oghuzs. The dynasty began to appear in history in 1340 when it was under the rule of Tur Ali Bey. The real founder of the state was Karayuluk Osman Bey who first established an alliance with Kadi Burhaneddin against the Kara Koyunlus, and then, soon after he fought off the Kara Koyunlu attacks, he killed Kadi Burhaneddin. He established an alliance this time with the Memluks against the Ottomans. His army was destroyed by Timur who had entered Anatolia. He then settled in Anatolia with Timur's help and support.

Uzun Hasan Bey (1453-1478), one of Osman Bey's sons, defeated the Kara Koyunlus and Timurids and took control of one part of eastern Anatolia and Persia. He became the adversary of the Ottomans in the west. He supported the Karaman Principality against the Ottomans. He also attempted to establish an alliance with the Crusaders against the Ottomans. After that attempt, the Ottoman Sultan Mehmed II defeated Hasan very harshly in the Battle of Otlukbeli. The Ak Koyunlu Dynasty did not recover after that battle. Hasan died in 1478. After his death there emerged struggles for the throne which resulted in the Safavid ruler Shah Ismail ending the Ak Koyunlu Dynasty.

## 3. The Kara Koyunlu (Qara Qoyunlu) Dynasty

The Kara Koyunlu Dynasty was founded in the second half of the fourteenth century in Erciş, on the coast of Lake Van, on the land extending from Erzurum in the north to Mosul in the south. The founder of the state was Bayram Hoca, the chief of the Karakoyunlu Turkmens. The Kara Koyunlu Dynasty was strengthened in the region by joining other Turkish tribes. The Kara Koyunlu Dynasty began in time to dominate all of Persia and Azerbaijan, except for Khorasan. By ending the Mongols' domination in the region, they played an important role in Azerbaijan becoming Turkish.

After Bayram Hoca's death, his successor Kara Mehmed (1380-1389) defeated the Artuqids. As a result of the struggle with the Timurids, Tabriz was seized and made the capital city. In the time of Kara Yusuf (1389-1420), who came to power after Kara Mehmed, the Kara Koyunlus continued their struggle with the Timurids. In the end of this struggle, Kara Yusuf fled from Timur and took refuge with Ottoman Sultan Bayezid I. This became one of the main reasons for the Ankara War. Yusuf recovered the state after Timur's death. He ended the Artuqids in 1409. In 1415, he seized Baghdad and completely removed the Timurid authority from Azerbaijan.

With Kara Yusuf's death in 1420, internal fighting began amongst Kara Yusuf's descendants. This weakened the Kara Koyunlu Dynasty. Meanwhile, on the outside, they were twice defeated by the Ak Koyunlu Dynasty in 1457 and 1467. In 1469 the Kara Koyunlu Dynasty completely disappeared from history.

## 4. The Safavid Dynasty

The Safavid was a Turkish state founded in Persia in the beginning of the sixteenth century. The name of the state came from Safiyuddin, a leader of the religious sect called Safavidye. Although the Safavid were at first a religious sect, later it became a political dynasty. The Safavids remained Sunni until 1392 but after that date they became Shiites.

Safiyuddin's sect spread throughout Anatolia, Persia, and Iraq. Even the Ottoman Sultans, Timur and the Ak Koyunlus were interested in it for a time. Timur Khan even gave Hoca Ali, one of Safiyuddin's grandsons, the city of Erdebil and gave him the right to behave independently there. Sheik Cuneyd, another grandson of Hoca Ali, separated from the sect of his predecessors through the influence of the Batini sect (an esoteric sect of Shi'i Islam). Taking advantage of the interest and respect shown to the Safavids during his grandfathers' time, he became involved in politics. Having arranged a rebellion against the Kara Koyunlu Dynasty, he had to desert his homeland and take refuge with Ottomans and the Karamans. By continuing with the same attitude however, he could not hold on to these places. He tried to found a principality in southern Anatolia and Syria by spreading his views among the Turkmens there. He came face to face however, with the Memluk obstruction there. The Ak Koyunlus established kinship with him by way of marriage to take advantage of his influence. Nevertheless, the Safavids could not found an independent administrative structure until Ismail came to power in 1499.

In 1499 Ismail became the leader of the Safavids and gathered around him the Turkish tribes in Anatolia that were under the influence and control of the Safavid. In 1501 he defeated the Ak Koyunlu Dynasty and seized Tabriz. He declared himself Shah, and founded the Safavid State making Tabriz its capital city. In 1509 he occupied Baghdad. He then moved towards the Ottomans in the West. To cause the Ottoman State to collapse from the inside, he sent Shiite propagandists with the title 'caliph' to Anatolia to arouse a religious and political rebellion against the state. These so-called caliphs became so influential that one of them, Shahkulu, initiated a rebellion. This rebellion was barely quenched by the Ottoman State.

Selim I, who came to power in 1512 in the Ottoman State, was aware of the Safavid threat. Thus, he set an expedition to Persia in 1514 to end that threat, and in the same time he terribly defeated the Safavids in the Battle of Caldiran. Afterwards, the Ottomans entered Tabriz and seized eastern Anatolia, Azerbaijan, and Diyarbakir. After the defeat of Caldiran, Shah Ismail did not do anything else against the Ottomans. Shah Ismail died in 1524. In the time of his successor Tahmasp (1524-1576) the struggle against the Ottomans was resumed. With the Treaty of Amasya signed in 1555, the Ottoman-Safavid struggle came to an end.

The Safavid State began to collapse in the middle of the seventeenth century. Different groups in the country tried to separate from the central authority by rebelling against the state. Nadir Shah, taking advantage of this chaotic situation ended the Safavid Dynasty in 1736 and founded the Afsharid Dynasty.

# CHAPTER 10

## The Ottoman (Osmanlı) Empire (1299 - 1922)

Ottoman history is conventionally divided into four periods: The Classical Age (1299-1600); Consolidation (1600-1774); Decline (1774-1914) and Dissolution (1914-1922).

### A. The Classical Age (1299 - 1600)

The term "Ottoman" is derived from the name of the Dynasty's founder, Osman ("Ottoman" in English). The Ottoman Dynasty was a member of the Kayı tribe of Oghuzs Turks (Turkmen) who began to move towards Iran in the ninth century. They settled in Merv in the Khorasan region with the Seljuk people, and with the Kayı who were forced to migrate towards Azerbaijan. In eastern Anatolia they settled with other Turkish tribes. Some parts of the Kayı people settled first in the area west of Ankara in the middle of the thirteenth century. Then they settled in the Sogut and Domanic environs, on the borderlands of the Byzantine Empire, which had been given to Ertugrul Ghazi, the leader of the Kayı, as an *ikta* by the Sultan Alaaddin in 1231. This territory roughly corresponded with the Roman province of Bithynia, which the Seljuks had taken from the Byzantines a century before. Osman Bey was made bey (commander) with the concord of all other Oghuz Tribes. He settled on the frontier with Byzantium when Ertugrul died in 1281 or 1288. Osman married the daughter of Sheikh Edebali, who had been a great spiritual master. This gave Osman the power to build his authority over the community. Shortly afterwards he captured the area stretching from Eskishehir up to the frontier of Bursa and Iznik. He established a friendly relationship with the Byzantine tekfur (ruler of a town or locality in Anatolia or Rumelia). Though Osman declared his frontier principality independent from the Anatolian Seljuk State in 1299, he recognized the Sultanate of Ilkhanate as his master.

During this time, many Turkish tribes were escaping from the Mongols and heading towards Anatolia where it was much safer than in western Turkistan. When the Mongol threat decreased in the second half of the thirteenth century, many Turkish principalities appeared in central and northwestern Anatolia. The Karaman principality, which was the strongest, claimed to be the successor of Seljuk. The other principalities were the Hamid, the Germiyan, the Aydin, the Karesi, the Menteshe, the Saruhan, and the Candar. They were primarily occupied with fighting each other in order to enlarge their individual territories.

*Osmanbey*

Keeping themselves out of the struggle over the throne of the Anatolian Seljuk State, the priority of the modest Ottomans was to fight against the Byzantines. It should be noted that this gave the Ottomans a great advantage in their fighting with the Byzantines rather than with their consanguine principalities. Most of the Turkish warriors who had escaped from Mongol cruelty in Turkistan at the end of thirteenth century participated in the Ottoman holy war against the infidels (*ghaza*) with great enthusiasm. Another advantage of the Ottoman principality was the weaker position of the Byzantines, which created a suitable atmosphere for Ottoman expansion westwards. Many Christians under Byzantine rule did not resist the Ottoman raids, as they seemed to have been happy to pass under the rule of an expanding polity with relatively light taxes. During this time Osman Bey was in a position to cooperate with the indigenous people of the region, even with some of the Byzantine tekfurs. One of these tekfurs, Mikhail, later converted to Islam.

The Ottomans abandoned the practice of dividing their territories among different heirs, as the nomadic Turkish states had done. This practice had caused bloody struggles for the throne among siblings which had caused these states to disintegrate in a short time. This seems to be the one of the main reasons why a weaker principality like that of the Ottomans was able to grow over the next century into one of the greatest empires not only in Turkish or Islamic history, but in world history.

The Ottoman principality first appeared after the defeat of the Byzantines at the Battle of Bafeus in 1302. Osman Bey captured a few fortresses near Bursa after a series of campaigns against the Byzantines, taking advantage of their inferior position and weaker authority. In 1320 he appointed his son Orhan, as commander of the army. Orhan's mission was to capture Bursa and Iznik. When Orhan entered Bursa in 1326, Osman was about to die. Orhan moved his capital to Bursa from Bilecik and continued to expand Ottoman holdings at the expense of the Byzantines. Particularly important for Orhan was the conquest Iznik (Nikaia), which the Anatolian Seljuks had lost in the First Crusades in 1096. He conquered Iznik in 1331. Two years later, the Byzantine emperor had to agree to pay tribute for the rest of his lands in Anatolia. The Ottoman principality began to transform into a state since (apart from its achievements) the authority of the Ilkhanate was dissolved.

Byzantium lost its last territory in Anatolia when the Ottomans conquered Izmit (Nikmedaia) in 1337. In 1345 Orhan put an end to the Karesi principality which was located in the Chanakkale and Marmara regions. This enabled the Ottomans to establish a permanent presence on the European side of the Dardanelles. Thus Suleyman Pasha, the son of Orhan Ghazi, gained control of the Gallipoli Peninsula in 1354. After Suleyman Pasha's death in 1357, he was replaced by Murad (the son of Orhan). Murad took control over Edirne (Adrinople) in 1361 and completed the conquest of all eastern Thrace. As the Ottomans expanded into the Balkans, they followed a settlement policy which made it clear that they were not just raiding and looting. They took control of the Balkans not only by force, but also by applying a conciliatory and peaceful method of diplomacy in which the Ottoman guaranteed non-Muslims security over their lives, possessions, and freedom of religious practices. This policy secured the loyalty of the indigenous peoples, who had been under heavy political and religious pressure from the previous feudal authorities.

As part of the settlement policy, Yuruks and Turkmen with no land to cultivate in Anatolia were settled in the occupied Balkan areas where they established villages and farms. This migration completed the turkification processes in the regions of eastern and western Thrace, Macedonia, Dobruzha and Deli Orman (Lodogorie).

### Sultan Murad I

The Ottomans entered the field of macro-politics during the reign of Murad I (1359-1389). During Murad's reign the Ottoman principality was transformed into a state with expanding frontiers as the Turks continued to advance into the Balkans. This necessitated the reorganization of state institutions in order to keep the expanding Ottoman territories intact. The first two Ottoman rulers, Osman and Orhan were ordinarily never referred to by any title grander than *Bey* or *Ghazi*. This was because: a) they were still dependent on Ilkhanate (even though this dependency was a mere formality); and b) they could not yet organize a state. Murad was the first Ottoman ruler to take the royal title of *Hünkar* and *Sultan*.

The Ottomans had developed a force of cavalry officers (sipahi) supported by timars. The timar was a form of land tenure, consisting of land grants or revenues by the Ottoman Sultan to an individual in compensation for his services, especially military services. The timars were necessary because state expansion could not be carried out on voluntary bases anymore. Another army group that was established by Murad I was a slave-infantry corps, called the Janissaries (*Yeniçeri*). The Janissaries also became the sultan's new bodyguards (the *Kapıkulu*). The Janissaries were periodically recruited through levies (*devşirme*) of boys from non-Muslim Ottoman subjects, independent of the fortunes of war. Thus was created a slave elite whose values for the Ottoman state quickly became apparent. The Janissaries and *Kapıkulu* played a crucial role in the survival and reunification of the Ottoman state in 1413. This is because their identity and status depended on the power of their Ottoman masters. Some administrative regulations (other than military ones) were also made in the state, like the establishment of two *Beylerbeyis* (Commander of Commanders, or, Governor General): one in Anatolia and the other in Rumelia, (the part of the Ottoman State which was in Europe).

When Murad I captured Filibe (Plovdiv), Pope Urbanus V urged for a Crusade in order to stop the Ottoman advance through the Balkans. The spirit of the Crusades was still alive, though it grew weaker. Those states in southwestern Europe that soon had to confront the Ottomans agreed. Turkish troops defeated the Crusaders in Bulgaria, Serbia, Hungary and Eflak (Wallachia), and Bosnia - first in *Sırpsındığı* (Chernomen), and then in Kosovo in 1389. Sultan Murad I was assassinated after the war by a Serbian nationalist, Milosh Obilich. The Kosovo War left no power other than Hungary capable of contesting the Ottomans south of the Danube River. When Sultan Murad I died, the Ottomans' territories covered over 500 thousand km squares. Thus the Ottomans, who had already transformed from a principality into a state with their new institutions, were preparing to become an empire.

## Abortive Efforts
## at Building an Empire

Back in Anatolia, the Turkish principality that was under the Ottoman sovereignty rebelled when they heard that Sultan Murad had died. In 1392 the Sultan Bayezid I (1389-1402) (he was the son of Murad, and was called *Yıldırım - thunderbolt*) annexed the principalities of Saruhan, Aydin, Candars, Menteshe, and Germiyan in Anatolia. Bayezid I maintained

*Mehmed II*

Murad I's expansion policy in the Balkans. Bayezid I defeated Eflak in 1391, he captured Thessalonica and besieged Istanbul in 1391 in order to unite his territory by putting an end to the Byzantine Empire. Another Crusade led by the Hungarian king Sigismund moved towards Nigbolu (Nikopol) in order to expel the Turks from the Balkans and rescue Istanbul. Yet in 1396 the Ottomans once again defeated the Crusaders at Nigbolu. Thus it became obvious that there was no power left in Europe which could come to Byzantium's aid. This achievement earned Bayezid I fame in the Islamic world.

Eliminating any threat that may have been directed against him, Bayezid I turned towards the Principality of Karaman with the confidence gained in Nigbolu to cement Turkish unity. To do so he first annexed Karaman in 1398, and then expanded his eastern frontiers up to the Middle Firat (Euphrates) by annexing Malatya (Melitene in Latin) and Elbistan, where the Memluks were stationed. By annexing all the Turkish states in central Anatolia and parts of western Anatolia, Bayezid I centralized the state and put an end to the vassalage system. Consequently, he used the title of Sultan of Rum (Anatolia), which had been the Seljuk Sultans' title. This meant that he claimed to be a successor of the Seljuks.

Bayezid's achievement was short-lived however, as Timur assaulted the Ottomans in 1402. Timur had founded a powerful empire in Turkistan and was expanding westwards. He claimed to be the heir of the Seljuks and the Ilkhanate. Timur saw the

Ottomans as a frontier principality that was dependent on him. Living at the same time as Timur (who had never been beaten by any power) may be seen as a misfortune for Bayezid, even though he ruled over a state that covered a million square kilometers and had achieved great victories against the Crusaders. When the two proud rulers became neighbors, a conflict seemed inevitable as they both had huge self-confidence. The brewing conflict exploded when Ahmed, the ruler of Celayirli, and Kara Yusuf, the ruler of Karakoyunlu, took refuge in Bayezid. Timur took advantage of this opportunity provided by the provocations of some displaced beys who fled to him.

## Hiatus (1402 - 1413)

Timur defeated and captured Bayezid and his two sons, Musa and Mustafa, in Ankara in 1402. Timur attempted to restore the other principality, which meant that the Anatolian frontier was pushed back from the time of Murad I. The Ottoman state that had to recognize Timur's superiority was on the verge of collapsing with this defeat, and lost its claim of being a great power. Sultan Bayezid could not stand being prisoner, though Timur treated him reasonably well. When Timur left Anatolia, the Ottoman territory was divided among Bayezid's three sons: Suleyman took control in Edirne, Mehmed took Amasya, and Isa took Bursa.

According to the Turkish system of succession (which dated from the ancient period in Central Asia) all the members of the ruling family had an equal claim to the throne. Even the Turkish states had been divided among the sovereign's family. The Ottomans however, had abandoned this practice at a very early point in their history. The Ottomans also refused to accept partnership in government in order to avoid any territorial fragmentation and bitter succession struggles. To prepare a young price (*Shehzade*) to become the new sovereign of the Empire, the current Ottoman sovereign would assign him to a provincial governorship. These procedures were legalized by Mehmed II, but they had been practiced since the time of Murad I.

These changes in administrative procedure were one of the main causes behind the ensuing civil war that lasted eleven years (1402-1413), which is called the Hiatus Era. In the end, Mehmed I carried out the unification of the Ottoman State and acceded to the Ottoman throne in 1413. Even though Ottoman authority was weakened during the Hiatus Era, much of the Balkans remained loyal to the Ottomans. After eliminating his brothers, Mehmed I avoided provoking the Byzantines and the Crusaders in order to be able to re-annex the Anatolian territory that had been lost in the Battle of Ankara. Thus he re-united part of the territories that belonged to the principality and lessened Karaman's influence in Anatolia. Then Mehmed I put down the rebellions of sheikh Bedreddin and Mustafa Çelebi, his brother. When he died in 1421, Murad II inherited a re-organized state that had regained its strengthen after 1 years of turmoil.

## Re-attempting to Rebuild an Empire

Sultan Murad II first struggled with the rebellions of his uncle Mustafa Çelebi, and his younger brother Mustafa. He defeated these rebellions with a great difficulty. Then he besieged Istanbul as the Byzantine Empire was experiencing an internal power struggle. His next goal was to strengthen Ottoman rule in the Balkans, where it had been weakened. In 1430 Thessalonica was seized and Hungarian influence over Serbia and Eflak was removed. The failure of the Ottoman's siege of the strategically important city of Belgrade in 1440, encouraged the Hungarians to attack the Ottomans. Hungary achieved some important victories, which made Murad II follow a conciliatory foreign policy. He signed an agreement with Hungary by which the Ottomans guaranteed not to cross the Danube River. Now that no threat remained for the state, Murad II left the throne to his son Mehmed. The Byzantines and the Hungarians saw this as a great opportunity for preparing a Crusade in order to remove the Turkish threat. They soon realized that they were mistaken, as the Crusaders were defeated at Warna in 1444 by the Ottoman army headed by Murad II (who had returned when the threat became apparent). John Hunyad made one more attempt, but was defeated again in 1448. These victories strengthened Ottoman authority south of the Danube River, and the Crusaders lost their hope of rescuing Istanbul from the Turks.

In Murad II's time, the capital city of Edirne became a center of culture and science. The scientific and cultural activities of the Anatolian principalities were moved there. When he died in 1451, Mehmed II inherited a powerful state from his father, as the Crusaders had been neutralized and the adverse effects of Timur's invasion were eliminated. The Ottoman frontier was now where it had been prior to the Battle of Ankara.

# Sultan Mehmed II: Building a Worldwide Empire

When Mehmed II acceded to the throne there was no serious threat directed against Ottoman unity. Taking previous experience into account however, Mehmed II saw Byzantium as a serious threat to Ottoman unity. Even though Byzantium had been living under Ottoman blockade for long time, the Byzantine emperors were provoking succession struggles among the members of the Ottoman Dynasty and were also calling on Crusaders for aid. His main objective was to build a centralized administration in which there should not be left any force which might have threatened the unity of the Ottoman Empire. He saw Byzantium as a major obstacle to this goal. It should also be remembered that most of the Muslim and Turkish conquerors' objective was to take Constantinople, not only because of its vast strategic and symbolic significance but also because of a saying of Prophet Muhammad's which sanctified the goal of conquering this city. Sultan Mehmed II's objective was to centralize the Ottoman state by removing the influence of any dynasties in Anatolia and any powerful families, such as the Çandarlı, whose members had been appointed as grand vizier since Murad I. Mehmed II also sought to remove the princes, who might have threatened the strength and existence of the Ottoman dynasty.

While preparations for the conquest of Constantinople were being made in 1452-1453, the Grand vizier Çandarlı Halil Pasha tried to dissuade Sultan Mehmed II from besieging the city. Çandarlı Halil Pasha argued that any action taken against the Byzantines would provoke more Crusades. He did not convince Sultan Mehmed II. Mehmed II had Urban (who was of Hungarian origins) prepare cannons to demolish the Byzantine ramparts and built the Castle of Rumelia on the European side of the Bosporus in order to prevent the Venetian navy from helping the Byzantines. Constantinople, now Istanbul (but the Ottomans continued to use the previous name for a long time) was finally conquered on May 29, 1453. Sultan Mehmed was given the title of *Conqueror* (*Fatih*). The Ottomans were now a world power.

After having conquered Istanbul, the Ottoman sultans could claim to be the heirs of the Roman Empire. Pope Pius II accepted this claim. He wrote to the Conqueror that all it would take to make him "the greatest man of your time by your universal consent was a little water with which you may be baptized". The Conqueror rejected this invitation to convert to Christianity, as his aim was not only to expand his power towards the west. His fundamental aim was to build a world-wide empire, or New Word Order, based on the happiness of humanity as defined by Islamic teachings and Turkish traditions. This fundamental aim of the Conqueror was shared by all previous and future sultans.

The conquest of Istanbul unified the Ottomans' territories and cemented the status of their empire as the preeminent power in southeastern Europe, the eastern Mediterranean and the whole Black Sea. The capital of the empire was moved from Edirne to Istanbul shortly after the city was conquered. It should be noted that one of the results of the conquest of Istanbul was the preservation of a world capital that was about to perish. The city remained the ecclesiastical center of the Greek Orthodox Church, of which Mehmet II proclaimed himself the protector. Mehmet II also appointed a new patriarch in the custom of the Byzantine emperors. Mehmet II regarded himself as the direct successor of the Byzantine emperors. He removed any dynasties that could make a claim to the Byzantine throne, such as David Comnenos in Trebizond, and Dimitrios and Thomas in the Morea (Achaia) Peninsula. Dimitrios and Thomas were the brothers of the last Byzantine emperor. The Conqueror sized Morea and put an end to the rule of Dimitrios and Thomas in 1460. He annexed Trebizond in 1461. This provoked a war that lasted sixteen years between the Ottomans and Venice. This war was prolongated due to the weaknesses of the Ottoman navy. During this time, Venice allied itself with Akkoyunlu rather than with Hungary and Albania. Mehmed II, whose empire was encircled from east and west, campaigned against Albania twice in 1466 and 1467. Uzun Hasan, the ruler of Akkoyunlu, allied himself with the Principality of Karaman and the Knights of Cyprus and Rhodes. He sought to expand towards Central Anatolia. Mehmed II annexed Karaman in 1468, and then subjugated Hasan by defeating him at the Battle of Otlukbeli in 1473. Thus the most important threat from the east was neutralized.

One of the most important achievements of Mehmed II was to restore Ottoman power over other Turkish states in Anatolia and remove any threat that might have come from the east. He also annexed territories on the Black Sea cost and brought the Crimean Khanate under Ottoman control. Thus the Black Sea became a Turkish Lake. Having lost one of its most important allies, Venice was forced to sign an agreement with the Ottomans in which they abandoned Shkodra and the islands of Limnos

(Limni) and Evia (Egriboz), and consented to pay tribute. Mehmed II's last campaign was against Italy. He wished to conquer Rome, the capital of the Western Roman Empire, as he saw himself a genuine heir to the entire Roman Empire. Otranto was seized in 1480, but the conquest of Italy could not be materialized as the sultan died in 1481.

Mehmed II's major aim was to form a centralized empire. He did so by eliminating any member of the dynasties that might claim a right to the throne, and any influential aristocrat or privileged class that might became an alternative power. The execution of grand vizier Halil Pasha might be seen as part of this policy. He also nationalized some private lands in order to decrease the aristocrats' power and improve the Empire's financial conditions.

### Solidifying the Empire under the Shadow of a War of Succession

The practicing of killing the brothers and sons of a prince when he ascended to the throne was legalized by the sultan. This was done in order to avoid rebellions and rival claims to the throne. This policy was intended to facilitate the Ottomans' realization of a New World Order (*Nizam-ı Alem*). When Mehmed II died he had two sons, Cem and Bayezid who contended for the throne. Most statesmen were in favor of Bayezid. Others, like Grand Vizier Karamani Mehmed Pasha, supported Cem. In the end Bayezid II succeeded his father. The Ottoman statesmen however, were already divided into two factions. The Janissaries killed Karamani Mehmed Pasha because he supported Cem, who had declared himself a sultan in Bursa. Cem proposed to his brother that they divide the empire in two: one part in Anatolia and the other in Rumelia. This idea was decisively rejected. A war between the two brothers' armies became unavoidable. Cem's army was defeated at the Battle of Yenishehir Plane on June 20, 1481. He then fled to Konya, and later to Egypt. Cem returned to Anatolia when he was called by Karamanoglu Mehmed Bey, but was defeated again by Bayezid II. This time he took refuge with the Knights of Rhodes. From Phodes he went to go to Rumelia to begin a successionist struggle. Cem ended up a captive of the European states, including the Papacy, who used Cem to blackmail the Ottomans. Bayezid II made payments to his brother's captors.

After Cem took refuge with the Knights of Rhodes, the Sultan executed Gedik Ahmed Pasha. Gedik Ahmed Pasha had played a crucial role in re-establishing Ottoman authority in Anatolia. Then Grand Vizier Ishak Pasha was dismissed. Thus Bayezid II took an exclusive hold on power by removing the two pre-eminent people who had assisted him in his struggle against Cem. Yet owing to Cem's uprising, the sultan was obliged to follow more conciliatory policy in domestic and foreign affairs. He tried to satisfy those whose lands were confiscated by Mehmed II by giving them back their land and possessions. As for Venice and Hungary, the Ottomans wanted to avoid provoking them into another Crusade, as Cem was still their captive.

However, a territorial connection with the Ceriman Khanate, who was subjugated by Mehmed II, was formed by annexing Akkerman and Kili of Bogdan (which was of strategic importance for Black Sea trade). After the death of Cem in 1495, Inebahti, Modon and Koroni were captured after a series of wars with Venice between 1499 and 1503. Thus the Ottomans became the biggest naval power in the Mediterranean Sea. One of the Ottomans' greatest naval commanders was Kemal Reis. Kemal Reis was the savior of thousands of Muslims and Jews who were

*Suleyman the Magnificient*

being persecuted in Spain. With instructions from Bayezid II, Kemal Reis transferred a great number of Spanish Muslims to North Africa and Ottoman territory. The Ottomans opened their doors not only to Muslims, but also to Jews. Spanish Jews were brought by Ottoman to live in Ottoman territory.

During the reign of Bayezid II, the Ottomans had to deal with two threats: one from the Memluk Muslim state, and the other from the Safavid state. While the nature of the struggle with the Memluks was greatly based on political influence, the conflict with the Safavids included a sectarian and ideological dimension. Since the time of Sultan Mehmed II, the Ottomans had regarded themselves as the leaders of the Islamic world, therefore they felt ready to take an increasing role in that matter. When the Memluks interfered in the affairs of the Dulkadirids (a buffer state in the area of Marsh-Elbistan) the Ottomans began a campaign against the Memluks that lasted from 1485 to 1491. Neither side could claim victory. The relationship between the two countries later improved as the Memluks appealed to the Ottomans for aid against the Portuguese navy that had begun to dominate the Indian Ocean and the Red Sea in order to take control of the Asian Spice trade routes. The Ottoman navy and military troops joined the Memluk army in their fight against the outsider.

## Ottoman Sovereignty in the Islamic World

The threat of the Safavids was different in character from that of the Memluks. The rise of the Safavid Dynasty in Iran with Shah Ismail, had created state that was both strong militarily and ideologically hostile to the Ottomans. Shi'ism, the form of Islam favored by the Safavids, was also attractive to dissident forces within the Ottoman state, which rallied to support the new dynasty in Iran by the provocation of Shah Ismail. A series of Shi'i-inspired uprisings among the Turkmen tribes of eastern Anatolia in the last years of Bayezid II's reign gradually increased due to Safavid propaganda. The Turkmens' support of the Safavids was not only religiously sectarian, but also political as they were not happy with the taxation system that the Ottomans applied. Shah Ismail used these discontented elements to strain the Ottomans. Consequently, the Shahkulu uprising in southwestern Anatolia broke out in 1511. The fact that it was put down with great difficulty was criticized by prince Selim who had been in Trebizond as provincial governor, and who had a close watch on Ismail's activities. Selim thought that the precautions taken against Shah Ismail were far from satisfactory, and that a rigid attitude needed be taken.

Meanwhile a succession struggle amongst the sultan's sons erupted as Bayezid became quite old. Selim, who had the Janissarie's support, ascended to the throne in 1512 by overthrowing his father, despite of the fact that many statesmen supported Prince Ahmed. After consolidating his reign in Istanbul, Selim I (also known *the Grim* or *the brave*) began to negotiate for peace with the European states. He sought peace with the Europeans because his first priority was to deal with Shah Ismail, and then with the Memluks. During Selim's reign, the direction of Ottoman conquests changed from west to east. Selim I defeated the Safavids at the battle of Caldiran in 1514. Shah Ismail fled from the battlefield. Sultan Selim (whose aim was to destroy the Safavid state) advanced as far as Tabriz, but was forced to set back due to some disturbances within his army.

Eastern Anatolia was secured for a time, and the threat of religious separatism was removed. The Ottomans also seized the most important trade centers of Tabriz-Aleppo and Tabriz-Bursa on the Silk Road. These provided great profits for the Ottoman treasury.

Selim's annexation of the Dulkadirids in 1515 brought the Ottomans into direct contact with the Memluk Empire for the first time. During this time, the Portuguese destroyed the Arabic Muslim trade in the Indian Ocean and threatened the Muslim holy cities of Mecca and Medina. The rulers of these cities wanted to send an envoy to Selim I to appeal for help against the Portuguese, but the Memluk sultan did not allow it. Selim I was eager to take control of the Memluk holdings in order to secure the eastern trade route, which had changed at the expense of the Ottomans after the Portuguese dominated the Indian Ocean and the Red Sea.

Selim destroyed the Memluks politically and militarily, conquering Aleppo and Damascus in 1516, and taking Cairo in 1517. As well as bringing Syria and Egypt under Ottoman control, this campaign also added Holy sites to the empire, such as Hejaz. The sheriff of Mecca declared his obedience to the Ottomans and handed over the Holy Trust, which included the belongings of the Prophet Mohammed. This made Selim the most reputable leader in the Islamic world. The result of the Memluk's defeat was to hand over the Caliphate to the Ottoman sultanate. The Abbasid Caliphate in Baghdad had been under the protection of the Memluks in Cairo after they had been defeated the Mongols in 1258. As a matter of fact, Ottoman sultans had been using the title of Chalip since Murad I due to their belief that they must follow the Chaplip's example in securing the roads for Hajj (Pilgrimage to Mecca), the protection of holy cities, and expanding and protecting Islam.

One of the main aims of Selim the Grim was to dominate India in order to remove the Portuguese navy from the region. The Portuguese had been threatening the holy land of Islam as well as the Ottomans' traditional trade routes. However, the Egyptian campaign showed that the Ottoman navy needed to be strengthened. A shipyard was then founded in the Golden Horn after returning from the Egyptian campaign.

At Selim's death in 1520, the Empire stretched from the Red Sea to the Crimea, from Tabriz to Bosnia, and had become a major participant and contender in the international power politics of the day. Furthermore, substantial Turkish Muslim migration to the Balkans had begun to make permanent changes in the demographic and ethnic structure of that area.

## The Golden Age of the Ottoman Empire (1520 - 1566)

Suleyman I inherited the throne without any opponents, and started to rule a powerful Empire. He was the longest-serving sultan, reigning from 1520 to 1566. He is known in the West as *Suleyman the Magnificent*, to the Turks he is known as *The Lawgiver* (*Kanuni*) in recognition of his complete reconstruction of the Ottoman legal system. Suleyman was known as a fair ruler in the Ottoman Empire, and an opponent of corruption. He was also noted as one of the greatest Islamic poets. Suleyman was considered one of the pre-eminent rulers of sixteenth century Europe, a respected rival to the Holy Roman Emperor Charles V (1519-1556), Francis I of France (1515-1547), Henry VIII of England (1509-1547), Henry VIII of England (1509-1547), Sigismund II of Poland (1548-1572), and Ivan of Russia (1530–84). Under his leadership, the Ottoman Empire reached its Golden Age and became a world power.

After succeeding his father, Suleyman I had to deal with a revolt led by the Ottoman-appointed governor of Damascus who was provoked by Shah Ismail. After securing the Ottomans' eastern borders, Suleyman the Magnificent turn his attention to the West in order to remove two hindrances to Ottoman expansion: Hungary and Rhodes. Suleyman's priority was to conquer Belgrade, which had been unsuccessfully besieged twice by Mehmet II. The conquest of Belgrade was vital to eliminating the Hungarians, who remained the only formidable force blocking further expansion into Europe. Belgrade fell in August 1521 after a series of heavy bombardments from an island in the Danube. Belgrade now became one of the preeminent bases for the Ottoman army's further campaigns into Europe.

# Conquests in Europe

At this point Suleyman the Magnificent had to divert his attention to the island Rhodes. The Knights of Rhodes had given their support to people in Egypt and Syria who were opposed to the Ottomans. In the summer of 1522, Sultan Suleyman dispatched an armada of some four hundred ships to Rhodes. Many of these ships had been inherited from his father's navy. At the same time, Sultan Suleyman personally leading an army of one hundred men across Asia Minor to a point opposite the island of Rhodes. Following a brutal five month siege, Rhodes capitulated. Sultan Suleyman allowed the Knights of Rhodes to flee the island, and they formed a new base in Malta. Having thus eliminated all serious threats, Suleyman resumed his campaign in Eastern Europe, particularly in Hungary. He became a major player in European politics by pursuing a policy that destabilized both the Roman Catholic Church and the Holy Roman Empire. Suleyman's destabilization strategy ensured that the Ottoman Empire would remain a formidable power in Europe.

The purpose of the Hungarian campaign was not only to expand the Ottomans' territories, but also to cause friction between the Hungarians and other European states. While Suleyman was preparing the Hungarian campaign, Francis I of France (who had been defeated by the Holy Roman Emperor Charles V at Pavia) provoked the Ottomans into attacking the Habsburgs. This created a convenient opportunity to intervene in European politics. On August 29, 1526, Suleyman defeated Louis II of Hungary at the Battle of Mohac, and Louis II died. In its the Battle of Mohac, Hungarian resistance and central authority collapsed. Suleyman then entered Buda (Budin). He appointed John Zapolya to the crown, who was supported by the opponents of the Habsburgs. In opposition to Suleyman, some Hungarian nobles proposed that the Archduke Ferdinand of Austria should become the king of Hungary. Ferdinand was tied to Louis II's family by marriage. These anti-Suleyman Hungarian nobles citied previous agreements that stated that the Habsburgs should take the Hungarian throne if Louis II died without heirs. A three-sided conflict ensued as Ferdinand moved to assert his rule over most of the Hungarian kingdom. Thus two kings appeared in Hungary: Ferdinand in northwestern Hungary, and Zapolya in central Hungary and Transylvania. This was the

start of a perennial war between the Ottomans and the Habsburgs.

Three years later, Suleyman I waged a campaigned against Hungary to reassert Zapolya's primacy. Ferdinand did not dare fight the Ottoman troops who re-occupied Buda in 1528 and unsuccessfully laid siege to Vienna in the following autumn. In 1531, due to Ferdinand's re-invasion of Buda, Suleyman I resumed his campaign against Ferdinand. This time his aim was to have a pitched battle with both Ferdinand and his ally, the emperor Charles V. The Ottomans advanced into Austrian territory, but Ferdinand refrained from a pitched battle with the Ottomans. Then the Ottomans had to return to Anatolia to combat the Safavids. Suleyman made an agreement with Ferdinand, who consented to the kingship of Zapolya and paid tribute for those Hungarian lands which were held by him. The question of choosing a successor to the Hungarian throne reappeared when Zapolya died in 1540. In 1541 Suleyman's forces returned to Hungary as Ferdinand besieged Buda. This resulted in a three-way partition of the Kingdom: Most of present-day Hungary was annexed as a Buda Beylerbeyligi (provincial governorship). Zapolya's son was installed as ruler of the independent principality of Transylvania, which was a vassal state of the Ottoman Empire. Ferdinand claimed "Royal Hungary" in the north and northwest, temporarily fixing the border between the Habsburgs and the Ottomans. Ferdinand agreed to pay tribute to Istanbul. The struggle between the Ottomans and Hungary resurfaced several times during Suleyman's reign without any significant change to the borders. This struggle was not limited to the European continent, but also extended to naval battles in the Mediterranean Sea.

## Conquests in the East

Taking advantage of Ottoman engagements in Europe, the Safavids began to harass the Ottomans in the east. In fact, it was the Habsburgs who played an important role in revitalizing the animosity between the Ottomans and the Safavids in order to counter-balance the Ottoman-French alliance in the west. The Ottomans expanded their authority over Baghdad and Tabriz in 1533-1534. Consequently, the Ottomans brought under their control the Silk Road (which was of vital importance to the Ottoman economy) and the Spice Route of Baghdad-Basra. Attempting to defeat the Shah once and for all, Suleyman embarked on a second campaign in 1548-1549. The Shah avoided confrontation with the Ottoman army and chose to retreat, just as he had done in the previous conflict. With this campaign the Ottomans took Van and its environs as well as some forts in Georgia. In 1553, Suleyman I began his third and final campaign against the Shah which ended with the Amasya Agreement in 1555. With the Amasya Agreement the Safavids accepted Ottoman sovereignty over Baghdad, Tabriz, and eastern Anatolia. The state of war with the Safavids that had started in 1514 finally came to an end.

## Superiority in the Mediterranean

The Ottomans gave great importance to improving their navy since the time of Mehmed II. This became a major issue in Selim I's time, when the Portuguese navy became a dominant power on the Asian Spice Route. A turning point for the Ottoman navy came in 1517 when it was joined by Hizir Bey (also called Barbaros Hayreddin Pasha) who had conquered Algiers and declared himself sultan. In 1534 he was appointed as an admiral-in-chief (*Kaptan-ı Derya*) and charged with rebuilding the Ottoman fleet. The Ottoman navy soon equaled those of all the other Mediterranean countries put together. The strategically important fortress of Koron in Morea had been lost to Charles V's admiral, Andrea Dorea in 1532. Koran was recaptured in 1533, and Tunis was brought under Ottoman control. In 1535 however, Charles V won an important victory against the Ottomans in Tunis. In 1538 the Spanish fleet was defeated at the Battle of Preveza by Hayreddin Pasha. This secured the Ottomans' control over the eastern Mediterranean for 33 years. The Ottoman navy achieved some important victories in the Mediterranean against Spain, but was defeated at Malta in 1565.

The Ottomans had been closely watching the Portuguese activities in the Red Sea and Indian Ocean since the time of Bayezid II. In the 1530s they took control of the Gulf of Basra and the Red Sea from the Portuguese navy. All these Ottoman efforts were intended to secure the Indian trade routes. In 1538 an Ottoman fleet captured Aden. After annexing Basra in 1547, a new fleet was built. The Portuguese tried to hinder Ottoman hegemony in the Persian Gulf by building the fortresses of Muscat and Hormuz. Both of these fortresses were of strategic importance, as they controlled entry to the Persian Gulf. Piri Reis was appointed the commander of the Ottoman fleet in the Indian Ocean and the admiral of the fleet in Suez. With Piri Reis the Ottomans recaptured Aden from the Portuguese in 1549. Piri Reis besieged Hormuz after seizing Muscat in 1552, which the Portuguese had occupied since 1507. When his fleet was besieged in the Persian Gulf by the Portuguese navy, Piri Reis returned to Egypt. Piri Reis' successors could not put an end to Portuguese superiority in the Indian Ocean and the Persian Gulf. This was mainly because the Ottoman fleet consisted of galleys with short range cannons, while the Portuguese navy consisted of ships with long range cannons. Yet with these campaigns against the Portuguese, the Ottomans were able to prevent them from settling in Aden, the Red Sea, and the coast of the Persian Gulf. The Ottomans also took control of Yemen and the southern coast of Arabia.

When Suleyman the Magnificent died in 1566, the Ottoman Empire had extended its territory from the Arabian Peninsula to the Balkan Peninsula. This was not the end of Ottoman expansion, as the Empire continued to make new conquests until the middle of the seventeenth century. The Portuguese could not be defeated in the Indian Ocean, and from this emerged the beginnings of European world supremacy. Though the Ottoman navy dominated the Mediterranean, they could not compete with the stronger European navy in the Pacific. Trade in the Mediterranean had not declined, but the Ottomans could not benefit from the trade developing on the Atlantic route. The European economy, which had been far behind the Ottomans', was now growing at a much faster pace. No matter how Europe grew, the Ottomans were still the most powerful state in the world up to seventeenth century. That is the why the Ottomans might not have realized the worst signs of the developments inside and outside the empire. This does not necessarily mean that the Ottomans were totally unaware of the European awakening, as they had tried to stop the Portuguese in the Indian Ocean.

# Ottoman Conquests after Suleyman I

After Suleyman I, the Ottoman Empire was ruled by a series of incapable sultans. Selim II (1566-1574), the son of Suleyman, was the first Ottoman sultan who did not lead his troops in a campaign. Yet he was the man who formulated the empire's conquest policy, even though Grand vizier Sokullu Mehmed Pasha controlled much of the state's affairs. For instance, Mehmed Pasha was not in favor of conquering Cyprus because he thought that it might provoke a Crusade. Cyprus was finally taken from Venice in 1571. The Hejaz and Yemen expeditions were also successful. A naval crusade led by Spain and Italy to save Cyprus was calamitously defeated by the Ottomans at Lepanto (Inebahtı) in the same year. This further demonstrated the Ottomans' superiority in the Mediterranean, which had first been proven at Preveza in 1538. The Empire's shattered fleets were soon restored and the Ottomans maintained control of the Mediterranean.

During Selim's time, the Ottomans perceived Russia as a menacing figure after it had conquered Astrakhan in 1556. Russia had been growing stronger since the beginning of the sixteenth century. A plan had been elaborated by Sokullu Mehmed Pasha to unite the Volga and Don rivers by a canal in the summer of 1569. This would have prevented Russia from expanding further south. By capturing the Khanates of Kazan and Astrakhan and the remnants of the Golden Horde, not only would the Safavids have been encircled via the Caspian Sea, but also the Central Asian trade routes lying to the west would be taken under Ottoman control. One of the aims of this project was to reach the Central Asian Sunni Muslims, whose collaboration might help the Ottomans against the Safavids. Another of Sokullu's projects was to open the Suez Canal in order to control the Indian trade route. These plans failed. The Ottomans reached the Caspian Sea in 1590 following a series of victories against the Safavids, but Ottoman authority only lasted for a short time.

After securing the eastern frontier, the Ottomans once again turned their attention west where problems had been brewing since 1587. The war between the Ottomans and Austria began in 1593 and took fourteen years to come to an end without any gain for the Ottomans. Austria organized a Crusade for the purpose of taking the vassal states of Wallachia, Bogdan and Transylvania from the Ottomans. Mehmed III (who had been forced to command his army) defeated the Crusaders at the Battle of

Keresztes (Hoçova) in 1596. During the Battle of Keresztes, the Sultan had to be dissuaded from fleeing the battlefield in the middle of the fight. The Battle of Keresztes did not bring an end to the Austro-Ottoman conflict, which continued until 1606. As the Safavids were attacking in the east, an uprising of Protestants in Transylvania forced both sides to sign an agreement in 1606, called Zitvatoruk. With this agreement the Ottoman sultans became the equals of the Austrian emperors. This was a major turning point in Ottoman foreign policy and diplomacy. Yet this period also marked the beginning of the end of Ottoman expansion, as the Habsburgs in Central Europe and the Safavids in Central Asia both set firm barriers against the Ottomans. Russia had also emerged as a strong power in the north that blocked Ottoman expansion.

## B. Crisis & Consolidation (1600 - 1774)

Ottoman conquests continued after the death of Suleyman I, though they gradually slowed down. There were some changes in the classical system of Ottoman administration after Suleyman I. For instance, while Ottoman sultans had traditionally commanded their troops into battle, Selim II (the son of Suleyman I) and his son Murad III (1574-1595), were both devoid of active military interests. In the late sixteenth century, the Ottoman Sultans abandoned the practicing of killing their brothers, yet they still distrusted filial loyalty. Mehmed III (1595-1603) was the last Ottoman Sultan who had his brothers killed, and who killed his son. The brothers of the Sultan were locked away in the harem of the palace. While they lived in luxury, they were forced to stay in small rooms in isolated conditions: this was called the cage (*kafes*) system. The traditional assignment of princes to provincial governorships to prepare them as future sultans was also abandoned. Sultan Ahmed I (1603-1617) introduced a legal code which stated that the oldest member of the Ottoman dynasty would ascend the throne.

At the beginning of the seventeenth century the Ottoman Empire was still the most powerful state in the world both in wealth and military capability. Yet the personal style of government cultivated among the earlier Sultans had completely disappeared as the result of the adjustments to the succession system. Once the sultans began coming to the throne without the practical preparations of a provincial governorship and bloody succession struggles, they were less able to dominate their own households and the affairs of the state. This decline in the Sultanate is regarded as one of the prime causes of crisis in the empire. As a result of the disintegration of the Sultanate, the real power in the Ottoman Empire moved elsewhere. Power struggles emerged among the various elements of the bureaucracy: the grand Vizier, the Divan, or Supreme Court, and especially the military (the Janissaries). This led to a constant shifting of power in the government. One should not forget the influence of the Sultans' mothers (*valide sultan*) on state affairs. They became a key link in factional networks starting with Hurrem Sultan, the wife of Suleyman I. With Hurrem Sultan the senior palace women (the sultan's mother and wives) acquired expanded influence that enabled them to make appointments to high ranking positions within the Empire. What the Ottoman Empire really needed at this time was a powerful sultan on the throne, as the empire faced grave social and economic problems.

During the second half of the sixteenth century the Ottomans began to experience an inflation problem. This was caused by the Ottomans' loss of hegemony over the traditional Asian trade routes to the Europeans. Demographic changes were another important cause of inflation: while the population rose dramatically, the cultivable lands of the empire (whose economy was mostly based on agriculture) did not expand. Devaluation raised the price of goods as the result of the rising population, and this increased the needs of the Treasury to finance a changing military system. Precious metals from America adversely affected the Ottoman economy as well.

The fact that the European monarchs gave great importance to using fire-armed infantrymen required that the Ottomans do the same. This had a transformative effect on the classical Ottoman military system. The financial system needed to accommodate this military policy. As infantry corps became a decisive factor in war, particularly with the Habsburgs, Ottoman statesmen had to recruit armed mercenaries from their subjected classes: these became known as the sekban infantry. The Ottomans also encouraged pashas and wealthy provincial nobles to recruit sekban infantryman to replace the *timarı sipahi* (cavalry). Parallel to the new recruitment of infantry, the Janissaries were growing in number (and declining in discipline and effectiveness). This placed another burden on the Ottoman economy. To meet their military expenditures, the Ottomans introduced a new land taxation system called "iltizam". Iltizams were sold off by the government to wealthy notables (*mültezim*) who would then reap up to five times the amount paid by taxing the peasants and extracting agricultural production. This created a discontentment among taxpayers who had to abandon their lands. The sekban infantrymen, whose wages were not paid during peace time, rebelled under the vigorous leadership of Jelalis. Peasants who had been dispossessed by the *iltizam* system also joined the rebellion. Many cultivated lands and villages were abandoned.

Back in Istanbul the Janissaries terrorized the officials and the people. The Janissaries became influential players in the government. This was mainly the result of the deterioration of the *devşirme* system. Throughout the seventh century, the Janissaries had slowly taken over the military and the important administrative posts in the government. The Janissaries passed these posts on to their sons, mainly through bribes. As they gained power, the Janissaries rebelled in Istanbul in order to bring their own men to the power, some times with the collaboration of valide sultans.

After Suleyman I, most of the Ottoman Sultans were too naive to overcome such problems. Osman II (1618-166), also called Genç (young) Osman, tried to restore the power of the sultans, but he was murdered by the Janissaries. He was succeeded by the 11 year old Murad IV, the son of Ahmed I. The young Murad IV remained for a long time under the control of his mother, the passionate Kosem Sultan. She essentially ruled through him. The empire fell into anarchy: the Safavids invaded Iraq, revolts erupted in northern Anatolia, and in 1631 the Janissaries stormed the palace and killed the Grand Vizier, among others. Murad IV feared suffering the fate of his elder brother, Osman II and decided to assert his power. Murad IV tried to stop the corruption that had grown during the previous Sultans, and that had not been checked while his mother was ruling through proxy. Murad IV succeeded in limiting wasteful spending in the government. He also banned alcohol and tobacco in Istanbul.

Murad IV most notable military achievement was a victory against the Safavids in which the Ottoman re-conquered Tabriz, Hamadan, and Baghdad in 1638. Murad IV himself commanded the invasions of Iraq and Iran, and proved to be an outstanding field commander. He was the last Ottoman Sultan to command an army on the battlefield. His campaign against the Safavids ended in 1639 with the signing of an agreement called the Kasr-i Shirin. During his expedition to Iran, he annihilated all rebels in Anatolia and restored order to the state. This did not last long, as he died at the age of 27. He was succeeded by his brother Ibrahim (1640-1648). The intrigues and revolts that Murad IV had placated during his reign began to reappear after his death.

Ibrahim was not capable of being sultan after he was released from the *Kafes*. He had not been educated for the task of ruling a great empire. Many historians believe that Ibrahim was mentally ill. His mental state might have been adversely affected by the long time he spent in the palace Kafes. Under Sultan Ibrahim reign, the Ottoman Empire quickly reached the verge of collapse. Ibrahim also threatened to bring an end to his family's dynasty, as he did not have a son. Fortunately, he finally had a son, Mehmed. This saved the empire's existence. Ibrahim at first stayed away from politics, but eventually he took power into his own hands and executed a number of viziers. This did not bring an end to the palace intrigues. Sultan Ibrahim was killed in a coup in 1648. Fortunately, while the Europeans were occupied wit h the Thirty Years' Wars (1618-1648), the Ottomans were able to struggle with the Safavids and other external problems without any threat from the West.

### The Köprülü Period

Mehmed IV (1648-1687) succeeded his father when he was only seven years old. Thus his grandmother, Kosem Sultan, acted as regent (1648-1651). This created a power vacuum: the state apparatuses, not surprisingly, were mostly controlled by the chief commanders of the Janissaries and the Sipahis, who had dominant roles in appointing viziers. The commanders terrorized the country and suppressed all of their opponents. The political and economic structure of the empire became very vulnerable. The struggle among senior palace women caused great damage to the state, as they took part in lobbying activities within the palace. The sustained clash between Kosem Sultan and Turhan Hatice Sultan (the mother of Mehmed IV) ended with the strangulation of the former. Turhan Sultan, who was not as passionate as her mother-in-law, became the regent. Shortly thereafter the commanders and their collaborators were hanged.

In the meantime, the Ottomans had invaded Crete in 1644 to retaliate for the capture of an Ottoman ship. The Ottoman ship had been sailing to Egypt when it was captured by Maltese corsairs in Crete. Hania, the second largest city in Crete, was conquered by the Ottomans. However, the war lasted longer as the mouth of Dardanelles and the ports of Morea were blockaded by the Venetians. In 1656 a huge panic was caused in Istanbul when a Venetian fleet defeated the Ottomans at the mouth of the Dardanelles, and then captured the islands of Tenedos and Limnos. Turhan Sultan searched for a wise man who could overcome the problems that the empire was experiencing. She appointed Köprülü Mehmed, an old man, as grand vizier in October 1656. Turhan Sultan then withdrew from imperial affairs. Mehmed IV, known as Avci (the hunter) as this outdoor exercise took up much of his time, gave up most of his executive power to his grand viziers. Thereafter the Köprülü family dominated politics and patronage for twenty-eight years. This period is called the time of the Köprülüs (1656-1683). For the first time in Ottoman history, a historical period was named after a grand vizier rather than a sultan.

During the time of Köprülü Mehmed Pasha (1656-1661) and Köprülü Fazıl Ahmed Pasha (1661-1676) the Ottoman Empire returned to the glories of Suleyman I's time. The Köprülüs regained the Aegean islands from Venice and fought successful campaigns against Transylvania in 1664 and Poland in 1670-1674. They also succeeded in suppressing the revolts of the Janissaries. When Ahmed Pasha died in 1676, the Ottoman Empire was once again a stable and powerful empire. Kara Mustafa Pasha, the last member of Köprülü Family, succeeded Ahmed Pasha as grand vizier.

The Ottoman Empire had been providing military assistance to the Hungarians and to non-Catholic minorities in the Habsburg-occupied portions of Hungary. In 1681, Protestants and other anti-Habsburg forces led by Imre Thokoly, rebelled against Leopold I. The rebels called for Ottoman aid. The Ottomans recognized Imre as King of "Upper Hungary" (eastern Slovakia and parts of northeastern present-day Hungary), and decided to campaign against Austria. The capture of the city of Vienna had long been an important strategic goal of the Ottoman Empire, due to its inter-locking control over Danubean (Black Sea-to-Western Europe) southern Europe, and the overland (eastern Mediterranean-to-Germany) trade routes.

## The First Great Defeat

In September 1683 Ottoman troops commanded by Grand vizier Kara Mustafa Pasha besieged Vienna after defeating the Austrian army led by Charles V, the duke of Loraine. However, the Ottoman army was defeated by a Christian alliance led by the Polish king Jan Sobieski. The betrayal of Murad Giray, the Crimean Khan, was the main reason for the Ottoman defeat. Mustafa Pasha had asked Murad Giray to hinder Sobieski's advance on the Danube River, but he did not take any action against the Polish troops. The Battle of Vienna brought an end to the Ottoman Empire's hegemony in southeastern Europe. In 1684 a new Holy League was initiated by Pope Innocent XI, which was composed of the Holy Roman Empire (headed by Habsburg Austria), the Venetian Republic, and Poland. In 1686 the Holy League was joined by Russia. The Ottomans had to fight against the Holy League in various areas for sixteen years. The Holy League eventually won the war in 1699 and forced the Ottoman Empire to sign the Treaty of Karlowitz. Accordingly, the Ottomans ceded most of Hungary, Transylvania, and Slavonia to Austria, while Podolia passed to Poland. Most of Dalmatia passed to Venice, along with Morea. Russia had captured the Asov fortress during the war, and now extended its territory to the Black Sea.

The Treaty of Karlowitz marked the beginning of Ottoman decline in Eastern Europe, and made the Habsburg monarchy the dominant power in Central Europe. The Ottomans now had to struggle to reorganize their navy and army. They also had to rehabilitate the financial and administrative position of the empire in accordance with European state practices rather than their own traditions. One of the Ottomans' priorities was to regain the lands that they lost with Treaty of Karlowitz. To do so, they would conduct a series of wars with Russia, Venice and Austria. The Ottomans achieved some important victories in these wars.

## A Series of Wars for Regaining Lost Territories

Peter the Great's ambition of gaining Russian access to a warm water port made conflict with the Ottomans inevitable. Peter the Great aspired to take the Asov Sea, then Istanbul, and then the Bosporus Straits with an eye to the Mediterranean. The Ottomans wanted to restore their position in the Asov Sea. The impending conflict started when Peter the Great incurred the enmity of the Swedes during his campaigns in the north. Carl XII of Sweden had invaded Russia but was defeated at Poltava in 1709. To escape being taken prisoner, Carl XII sought asylum in Turkey, which was granted by Sultan Ahmed III (1703-1730). Through his ambassador, Tolstoy, Peter the Great demanded that he should be extradited, but this was rejected. Since the Russians insisted, Ahmed III had Ambassador Tolstoy thrown into the Prison of the Seven Towers (*Yedikule Zindanı* in Turkish) in Istanbul. That meant war between the two countries.

Ottoman troops decisively defeated the Russian army at Pruth on July 28, 1711. For some unknown reason, the Ottomans were not able to take advantage of this victory that could have enabled them to advance to Moscow. Instead, Peter the Great was forced by the terms of the Treaty of Pruth to withdraw the permanent ambassador to Istanbul and to cede the Asov Sea, which had been Russian since 1700. Thus the Ottomans regained their self-confidence by defeating one of the members of the Holy League. Then they turned their attention to Venice (which was in decline) and recaptured most parts of Morea. Knowing that it would be the next target, Austria formed an offensive alliance with Venice in 1716. Now the Ottomans, who were no longer winning, were forced to sign the peace treaty of Passarovitz in 1718 by which all of Morea was given to the Ottomans, and Belgrade and Timishoara (Temeşvar) were ceded to Austria. By losing Belgrade, the Ottomans' position in the Balkans became vulnerable.

## The Tulip Era (1718 - 1730)

Faced with these losses, Grand Vizier Damad Ibrahim Pasha (who had signed the Passarovitz Agreement with Austria) believed that the empire needed to carry out some reforms. These reforms would put an end to the losses and stop socio-economic and political corruption. He also proposed a policy of peace. Accordingly, this thought led to a new phase in Ottoman history from 1718 to 1730 which is called the Tulip Era (*Lale Devri*). The name of the period is derived from the fact that there was a tulip craze. Tulips were widely purchased by the nobility and came to represent the fashion of the era. During this era, Ibrahim Pasha sent representatives to European capitals in order to gain knowledge about the Western renaissance. A printing house was established in Istanbul in order to publish Turkish books. New libraries were opened and some western and eastern books were translated into Turkish. Unique Ottoman cultural and artistic artifacts saw a sharp increase throughout the empire. The capital had new housing projects, especially with the establishment of the Yalis on the Bosporus.

It was a relatively peaceful period and for the first time in their history, the Ottoman Empire oriented itself towards the West. This meant that the Ottomans began to realize European progress. Until this time, Ottoman statesmen had believed that the socio-economic and political corruption in the Ottoman Empire had been caused by the loss of classical Ottoman values (which were the only ways to escape corruption and internal disorder). With the Tulip Era however, it was believed that returning to past ways was not the solution. Instead, the Ottomans should assimilate European innovations. All this however, did not meet the people's needs. There were those who were in poverty while the ruling elite were living in luxury. Another important event that had raised the people's irritation was the Safavids' recapture of Tabriz. In 1730 an uprising of discontented people led by Patrona Halil broke out in the capital. Ahmed III was dethroned, Mahmud I (1730-1754) succeeded him, and the Grand vizier was killed. This marked the end of the Tulip Era. The reforms lasted a very short time.

Taking advantage of the situation that the Ottoman Empire faced, Catherine I of Russia (1725-1727) continued the policy of seeking access to the southern seas begun by her husband, Peter the Great. She allied herself with the Austrian Empress Anna (1730-1740) against the Ottomans. Initially Russia won splendid victories by taking Ochakov (Özü), in the Crimea in 1737. For the first time the Russians began to entertain the notion of taking Istanbul and re-establishing the ancient Byzantine Empire. The Ottomans however, recaptured Belgrade from Austria. Austria withdrew from the war and Russia had to sign an agreement with Istanbul, called the Belgrade Treaty, in 1739. Through the intercession of France, the Belgrade Treaty returned Belgrade and Serbia to the Ottomans from Austria. Russia agreed to demolish the fortress at Asov, and to not build up its navy in the Asov Sea and the Black Sea. The Russians thus lost the right to navigate on the Black Sea. They would henceforth be forced to carry on trade with Ottoman ships flying the Ottoman flag. In addition, the Ottoman Empire not only regained some of the territories that had been lost with the Karlowitz and Passarovitz agreements, but also gained the confidence of being able to fight two of the Great Powers at the same time.

After the Belgrade Treaty, the Ottoman Empire was inclined to keep peace and no longer considered war as the only possible solution to its foreign problems. This reflected the climate of the times, in which diplomacy had become the primary option in international relations. The Ottoman Empire followed this policy for thirty years. One of the biggest advocates of this policy was the Grand Vizier Koca Ragıp Pasha (1757-1763), who avoided making an alliance with any state against the others. After his death in 1763, the Ottomans retreated from that policy. This decision ended in tragedy. It was partly because Catherine II of Russia (1762-1796) pushed the Ottomans into war by revitalizing Russia's expansionist policy towards the Mediterranean. The war with Russia was followed by international tension within Poland, where there was strife between the nationalists and King Stanislaus Poniatowski, who had Russian military backing. The Russian troops pursued the Polish nationalists taking refuge in Ottoman territory. The Russians followed the Poles to the Ottoman town of Balta. In Balta the Russian troops massacred the Polish nationalists. This charge was denied by Russian authorities. Following this border incident at Balta, Sultan Mustafa III declared war on Russia on September 25, 1768 without any decent military preparation, as the Russian massacre had aroused a great reaction among the Ottoman people.

### The Russo-Turkish War (1768 - 1774)

It was a devastating war that lasted for six years and was fought both on land and sea. Russia was supported by the United Kingdom, who offered advisers to the Russian Navy. Hostilities commenced simultaneously in the Balkans, the Crimea, and on the Caucasian-Georgian border. A Russian fleet from the Asov Sea ravaged the Turkish Black Sea coast and even showed signs of forcing an opening through the straits. At the same time a second Russian fleet sailed from the Baltic to the Mediterranean, where it was supported by a British fleet under Admiral Elphinstone. The Turkish Mediterranean fleet was defeated by the Russian and British navies on July 5, 1770 in a clash at Chesme (Çeşme), one of the districts of Izmir.

These setbacks made the Turks urge for peace negotiations, but the Russians refused. The war dragged on and the Turks were able to drive the Russians back across the Danube in 1773, albeit not for long. Soon afterwards they attacked Dobruzha again, but failed to capture Silestre and Warna. During this conflict Mustafa III died on December 24, 1773. He was succeeded by Abdulhamid I (1774-1789). After a series of defeats, Abdulhamid I did everything in his power to save what he could. Eventually he was forced to sign an agreement, called the Treaty of Küçük Kaynarca (Kuchuk Kainarji), with harsh Russian terms on July 21, 1774.

## C. Decline (1774 - 1914)

The treaty of Küçük Kaynarca was a devastating agreement for the Ottoman Empire and marked the beginning of Ottoman decline in southeastern Europe and the Black Sea. With the treaty, the Russians secured the right to free navigation on the Black Sea, unobstructed passage into the Mediterranean, respectful treatment of their ambassadors, free access to the Holy Sepulcher for Russian pilgrims to Jerusalem, and protection for all Christians on Ottoman soil. This last concession generated severe conflicts, since this privilege had already been granted to the French by Suleyman the Magnificent. Moreover, the Ottomans lost the Asov Sea and had to renounce all claims to Walachia. The Ottomans also lost the Crimean Khanate, to which they were forced to grant independence. The Crimean Khanate, while nominally independent, was dependent on Russia and was formally annexed into the Russian Empire in 1783. The most significant aspect of this treaty to naval history is that it gave Russia access to warm water ports and passage through the Dardanelles.

Abdulhamid I sought ways of expunging the disgrace of the Treaty of Kaynarca. However, the Russian threat towards the Ottoman Empire continued to increase as Catherine provoked the Christians in the Balkans to rebel against the Ottomans. Russia also made an alliance with Austria in order to share the Ottoman territories and capture Istanbul. In the face of constant Russian provocation, the Ottoman Porte (*Porte* was used to refer to the Ottoman government) declared war against Russia on August 19, 1787. The desire to regain Crimea and Küçük Kaynarca from Russia was the Ottomans' main reason for declaring war. But the Ottomans' preparations were inadequate and the moment was ill-chosen, now that Russia and Austria were allies. Fighting against two great powers on two fronts put the Ottomans in great difficulty. Young sultan Selim III (1789-180 7) was anxious to restore Ottoman prestige with a victory before making peace, but the condition of his troops rendered this hope impossible. Luckily Sweden and Prussia, who were worried about the growth of Russia and Austria and the effects of French Revolution of 1789, had signed offensive treaties with the Ottoman Empire which brought an end to the war. The French Revolution rescued the Ottoman Empire. Austria ceded the territory that it had seized in the war with the Ottoman Empire (including Belgrade) and guaranteed not to make any alliances with Russia against the Ottomans in the Treaty of Zishtovi in 1791. The Treaty of Yassy in 1792 that was signed with Russia relieved Turkey of some of the burden imposed by the Treaty of Kaynarca. Nevertheless the Ottomans had to renounce their claim to the Crimea and Bessarabia. Yet at this time the Great Powers had more pressing problems than paying heed to the Ottomans. Their interests no longer lay in the east but in the west. In Paris the Revolution had triumphed.

## Efforts at Ottoman Military Reform

Ottoman authorities sought to improve their military according to Western standards since the beginning of the eighteenth century. In 1731 Mahmud I appointed Comte de Bonneval to organize the artillery division (*Humbaracı Ocagı*) of the Ottoman army in accordance with western models. Comte de Bonneval was a refugee in the Ottoman Empire and a convert to Islam. He later became known as Humbaraci Ahmed Pasha. A military school called *Hendesehane* was founded in 1734 in order to train military personnel for the artillery division. It rendered valuable services to the Ottomans in its war with Russia and Austria in the years 1736-1739. However, this school was closed in 1747, due to the opposition of the Janissaries. It is a fact that Ottoman statesman, including the sultans, had longed for radical reform in their military system. But these longings were frustrated by the opposition of the Janissaries, who had gone so far as to kill sultans. When the Russo-Turkish war of 1868-1774 ended in Ottoman defeat, Abdulhamid I revitalized the military reforms.

In order to compete with the European powers, Adulhamid I brought in many foreigners to serve as Ottoman military advisors, regardless of whether or not they were Muslim or committed to the Ottoman cause. One of the western reformists who was brought in was François Baron de Tott, a French officer. He succeeded in building a new foundry for making howitzers, and formed mobile artillery units. He built fortifications on the Bosporus and directed the construction of a new naval base. With the advice and initiative of de Tott, the Ottomans started a naval science course that laid the foundations for the *Mühendishane-i Bahri Humayun* naval school in 1775. In Selim III's time, the school for land forces, the *Mühendishane-i Berri Humayun*, was founded in 1795 in order to train the officers of the artillerymen in western styles.

Sultan Selim III believed that establishing a modern army in the Western style was the only way that the Ottoman Empire could regain its former power. After ascending to the throne, Selim III sent Ebu Bekir Ratıb Efendi to Vienna as his ambassador. Efendi's task was to prepare a report about the European powers, especially about the army and administrative formation of Austria. Later he launched a great deal of reforms in the fields of finance, commerce, administration, and the military. His reforms as a whole were called *Nizam-i Cedi*d, which means New Order. The most important change was the creation of an elite new infantry unit, the *nizam-i cedid*. The *nizam-i-cedid* was given western uniforms, weapons, and training. It achieved great successes in a short time by defeating the army of Napoleon Bonaparte at Akka (Acre) during his Egyptian campaign. This proved the importance of the new modern Ottoman army. This achievement brought them public support as well. This group, however, offended the Janissaries who had become conservative elite, using their military power to advance themselves commercially and politically.

Emboldened by this success, Selim III issued an order stating that in the future the Janissaries should be taken annually to serve in the nizam-i-cedid. Hereupon the Janissaries and other enemies of progress arose in Edirne. In view of their numbers (exceeding 10,000) and the violence of their opposition, it was decided that the reforms must be given up for the present. The Janissaries arose once more in revolt. They induced the Sheikh-ul-Islam (the superior authority in the issues of Islam) to grant a fetva against the reforms. The Janissaries also dethroned and imprisoned Selim III and placed his nephew Mustafa IV (1807-1808) on the throne. In 1808, he was replaced by Mahmud II (1808-1839). In the same year, martial law was introduced by Alemdar Mustafa Pasha, who restarted the reform efforts. His first action was to ally with the Janissaries to break the power of the provincial governors. He then turned on the Janissaries, massacring them in their barracks in Istanbul and the provincial capitals in 1826. Sultan Mahmud intended to replace the Janissaries with other regular troops, called *Asakir-i Mansure-i Muhammediye*. It is interesting to note that the Ottoman public called the massacre of the Janissaries *Vak'a-i Hayriyye* (The Favorable Event).

## The Ottoman Empire in the Nineteenth Century

The Ottoman Empire spent most of its energy defending its territorial integrity, which was being challenged by the nationalist movements backed by the great European powers. At the same time, the Ottoman Empire had to fend off European intervention in its internal affairs. To accomplish both of these goals, the Ottomans embarked on a series of reforms in the military, economic, and bureaucratic fields in order to modernize the structure of the empire. During the nineteenth century however, the Ottoman Empire encountered major crises involving the great European powers who provoked Ottoman subjects against the Porte.

The implications of the decline of Ottoman power, the vulnerability and attractiveness of the empire's vast holdings, the stirrings of nationalism among its subjected people, and the periodic crises resulting from these and other factors became collectively known to European diplomats in the nineteenth century as "the Eastern Question". In 1853 Tsar Nicholas I of Russia described the Ottoman Empire as the sick man of Europe. The problem from the viewpoint of European diplomacy was how to dispose of the empire in such a manner that no one power would gain an advantage at the expense of the others and upset the political balance of Europe.

The Ottoman Empire entered the nineteenth century with a serious crisis caused by Napoleon's invasion of Egypt in 1798. Selim III, who gave great importance to relationships with France (the Ottoman's long-standing ally), ascended to the throne just before the French Revolution. He even corresponded with Louis XVI and Napoleon Bonaparte. In fact, the French Revolution did not raise any reaction since it was seen as an internal problem of France. Besides, the Ottomans had no time to poke its nose into other states as had its own problems to overcome and its army was simultaneously struggling against two powerful states, Austria and Russia. The Porte did not analyze the effects of the French Revolution on the multi-ethnic Ottoman Empire. Thereafter the Ottoman Empire would become the victim of the Great Powers, whose politics were directed against its existence. Ottoman authorities were surprised however, when Napoleon invaded Egypt in 1798. It is not clear why Napoleon insisted on conquering Egypt. The ostensible aims were to gain control of the Indian Empire from the hands of the British. Napoleon's own memoirs list the reason solely as "glory". No matter what the motive was behind the invasion, its legacy put the Ottomans in great danger. First of all, the Ottoman Empire was not able to drive the French out of Egypt without the assistance of Russia and Great Britain, who had their own interests there. The French forces withdrew from Egypt and then Egypt became a battlefield of Great power politics.

Thus Ottoman authority in Egypt grew weaker. The eventual winner in what was effectively a civil war was Muhammad Ali. He was an Ottoman military commander, who had been present at the first battle of Abukir in 1799. After the French left, he was sent to Egypt as second in command of an Albanian contingent sent to support some of the most professional Ottoman troops. By 1805 he was in effective command of Egypt, and his position was recognized by the Sultan in Istanbul. For the next forty years, Muhammad Ali ruled Egypt almost as an independent state.

After leaving Egypt, the relationship between the Ottomans and the French was restored. This irritated the Russians and British. Great Britain threatened Istanbul by sending its navy into the Dardanelles while the Ottomans were fighting against Russia who had invaded Walachia and Bogdan in 1806. The Porte sought Britain's co-operation against Russia and signed an agreement in 1809. The second Russo-Turkish war, which lasted until 1812 ended with the treaty of Bucharest in which the Ottomans ceded Bessarabia to Russia, and some concessions were given to the Serbians who were in revolt.

## Nationalist Movements and Rebellions

In the early nineteenth century the Ottoman Empire was confronted with two problems. First, it had to counter the imperialist powers' attacks on its territories. Second, it had to struggle with the rebellions of its Christian subjects under influence of nationalist movements, which were triggered by the

French Revolution. The first nationalist rebellion in the Ottoman Empire occurred Serbia. The resistance of Serbian gangs who had complained about the applications of the Janissaries and the pressure of the *Ayans* (the provincial notable) acquired a nationalist character due to the misapplications of the Ottoman authorities in 1804. Russia, who had a cultural and religious affinity with the Serbs, supported them. In order to avoid provoking Russia, the Ottomans gave Serbia autonomy in 1816.

The Serbian movements however, stirred up the Greek revolt. The *Filiki Eterya* (The Friendly Society) was founded in 1814 with the purpose of overthrowing Ottoman rule in Greece and establishing an independent Greek state. By the first months of 1821 the *Filiki Eterya's* membership numbered around one thousand. Among its members were tradesmen, clergymen, executives of the Ottoman Empire from Fanari, and others. The Ottoman Empire was caught off guard when the Greek revolt began in Morea in 1821. It spread out towards central and southern Greece within a short-time. Sultan Mahmud asked his Egyptian governor for aid. Muhammad Ali Pasha agreed to send his army to Greece in exchange for Crete and the Peleponnesos, which the Ottoman Sultan agreed to hand over to Egyptian control. At this point, while the Greek revolt was about to be taken under control with Egyptian aid, the European powers intervened in favor of Greece.

The first nineteenth-century crisis to bring about European intervention was the Greek War of Independence. On October 20, 1827 the British, Russian and French fleets, on the initiative of local commanders but with the tacit approval of their governments, attacked and destroyed the Ottoman fleet, including the Egyptian one, at the Battle of Navarino. This was the decisive moment in the war of independence. While France and Britain remained silent, Russia seized Walachia and Moldavia once more, and Russian forces advanced as far as Edirne and the eastern region of Anatolia. The Peace of Edirne in 1829 ended the war. Russian merchant ships acquired free passage through the Dardanelles, Russia ceded the territories that it had acquired, and Greek independence was guaranteed. The Ottomans accepted the establishment of an independent Greek Empire. This event marked the beginning of the gradual break-up of the Ottoman Empire, as other non-Turkish peoples of the empire began their own independence movements.

## The Egyptian Question

Muhammad Ali had established a modern army and navy in Egypt with the help of France, who wanted to counter the British influence in the eastern Mediterranean area. When he was not rewarded as promised for his assistance during the Greek Revolt, he invaded Syria in 1831 and pursued the retreating Ottoman army deep into Anatolia. In desperation, the Porte appealed to Russia for support. Britain then intervened, forcing Muhammad Ali to withdraw from Anatolia to Syria. The price the sultan paid Russia for its assistance was the Treaty of Hunkar Iskelesi of 1833. Under this treaty, the Bosporus and Dardanelles straits were to be closed on Russian demand to naval vessels of other powers.

It is interesting to note here that the Ottoman Empire appealed for help to Russia against its own governor's revolt. This promoted the intervention of European powers in the internal affairs of the Ottoman Empire. France and Great Britain, who were anxious to see Russia penetrate the Porte, declared that they would not accept any modification to the status quo of the Turkish Straits (Bosporus and Dardanelles). Thus, in addition to the Egyptian question, the Straits question also came out. When the war resumed with Muhammad Ali in 1839, the five European powers, led by Britain (who was worried about Russian intervention) submitted a memorandum to the Porte in order to reach an agreement with Egypt. Thus an internal problem of the Ottoman Empire became an international question. After the Ottomans were defeated once more by Muhammad Ali, they signed an agreement with Britain called the Treaty of Balta Limanı, which gave Britain great economic and political advantages in exchange for its support of the Porte.

Under the London Convention of 1840, Muhammad Ali was forced to abandon his claim to Syria, but he was recognized as the hereditary ruler of Egypt under nominal Ottoman dominion. Under an additional protocol in 1841, the Porte undertook to close the straits to warships of all powers.

## Mahmud II and Civilian Reforms

Mahmud II carried out crucial reforms during his sultanate, despite the fact that the Empire was experiencing many critical external and internal problems. He began by destroying the Janissaries in 1826 as he saw them to be a barrier to enacting the needed reforms. Then he laid the foundations of the modern institutions of the Ottoman Empire. The sultan sent students to Europe in order to have modern military training. After founding military and medical schools, he brought instructors and specialists from Europe to increase the level of education. For the first time in Ottoman history, except for the brief Tulip Era, western influences appeared in Ottoman arts and culture. The clothing of officers and the Ottomans' administration were re-organized in accordance with European style. The Divan turned into a cabinet system. In another important series of measures, the administrative government was simplified and strengthened. A large number of sinecure offices were abolished, and the Sultan gave a valuable personal example of good sense and economy by re-organizing the imperial household, and mercilessly suppressing all titles without duties, and all salaried officials without functions.

The reforms of Mahmud II were seen by Ottoman historians as a project of transforming a civilization. Therefore, western historians compared him with Peter the Great of Russia (who carried out radical reforms) and called the sultan a "Peter the Great of the Ottomans." According to some Turkish historians, Mahmud II was the Greatest Ottoman sultan after Suleyman I, because his reforms laid the basis of the Turkish Republic.

### The Tanzimat Period (1839 - 1876)

*The Tanzimat*, meaning "reorganization" was a period of reformation that began in 1839 with the proclamation of a decree called the *Tanzimat Firman* by Sultan Abdulmecid (1839-1861). *The Tanzimat Firman* was prepared by Mustafa Reshid Pasha, who was a British sympathizer, and submitted to sultan Mahmud. After Mahmud died, and the new sultan approved the *Tanzimat*. The Tanzimat consolidated and enforced reforms that were initiated under Mahmud II. The Tanzimat guaranteed Ottoman subjects perfect security for their lives, their honor, and their property. It also guaranteed the equality of collecting taxes, the right of possession to everyone and the establishment of courts in order to defend those rights.

It might seem that the aim of the reforms was to have western support in the face of not only an external threat but also an internal one (as the example of the Muhammad Ali event demonstrated). This in fact was the case. It should not be forgotten however, that *the Tanzimat Firman* had already acknowledged the necessity of reforms long before the Tanzimat. What the Ottomans wanted was to prevent the dismemberment of the empire. Therefore, the reforms aimed to encourage *Ottomanism* among the secessionist nations and to stop the rise of nationalist movements within the empire. These attempts failed, despite their attempt to integrate non-Muslim and non-Turks more thoroughly into Ottoman society with new laws and reforms.

The European powers tried to take advantage of the *Tanzimat* for their own purposes. For them, the *Tanzimat* was an opportunity for interfering in the affairs of the Ottoman Empire. The European powers demanded that the rights of Christian subjects in the Ottoman Empire be expanded further. These Christian subjects might then be used to undermine the Ottoman Empire for the benefit of the European powers. According to the European powers, Christians in the Ottoman Empire did not have enough freedom and the Tanzimat did not meet their demands. Thus, the constant European pressure which had been put on the Ottomans forced the Porte to introduce new rights for non-Muslim subjects in 1856 with declaration of Reform Firman. The capitation tax, which imposed higher tariffs on non-Muslims was abolished; non-Muslims were allowed to become soldiers, and various provisions for the better administration of the public service and for the advancement of commerce were introduced. None of this satisfied the European powers, and they continued their pressure on the Ottoman Empire until it collapsed.

Great Britain began to penetrate the domestic affairs and foreign policies of the Ottoman Empire. Britain's position with the Porte had already been strengthened with the Treaty of Balta Limanı and its role in declaring the Tanzimat. Ottoman statesman, particularly Mustafa Reshid Pasha, believed that the Ottoman state would not be safe unless it eliminated the Russian threat. For this reason the Porte allied itself with Britain and France. This ill-calculated move came at a time when Russia put a series of unacceptable demands on the Porte, which led to a major war with Russia called the Crimean War (1854-1856). While the Ottoman Empire was preoccupied with the *Tanzimat* reforms, the European powers (except for Russia) were struggling with the rebellions of 1830 and 1848. These rebellions had attempted t o transform the European social order and the established boundaries of European states. Taking advantage of these rebellions in Europe, Russia moved in the direction of handling the Eastern question in its own favor.

Russia was primarily interested in acquiring territory. Throughout the seventeenth and eighteenth centuries Russia had slowly been annexing Muslim states in Central Asia. By 1854, Russia found itself near the banks of the Black Sea. Anxious to annex territories in Eastern Europe, particularly the Ottoman provinces of Moldavia and Walachia, the Russians went to war with the Ottomans on the flimsiest of pretexts: the Ottomans had granted Catholic France the right to protect Christian sites in the Holy Land (which the Ottomans controlled) rather than Orthodox Russia. That, according to the Russians, justified going to war with the Ottomans. France, Britain, and the Ottoman Empire formed an alliance against Russia. The three year Crimean War ended with the Treaty of Paris in 1856, in which Russia abandoned its claim to protect Orthodox Christians in the Ottoman Empire and renounced the right to intervene in the Balkans. Furthermore, the Tsar and the Sultan agreed not to establish any naval or military arsenals in the Black Sea. The Black Sea clauses came at a tremendous disadvantage to Russia, for this greatly diminished the naval threat it posed to the Turks. Moreover, all the Great Powers pledged to respect the independence and territorial integrity of the Ottoman Empire. It quickly became apparent however, that these were hollow words.

The Treaty of Paris stood until 1871, when France was crushed by the German states in the Franco-Prussian War. While Prussia and several other German states united to form a powerful German Empire, the Emperor of France, Napoleon III, was deposed with the formation of the French Republic. As the European balance of power shifted with the emergence of two powerful states in Europe, namely Italy and Germany, Russia denounced the terms of the Paris Treaty concerning the naval presence in the Black Sea. Then Russia decided to solve the Balkan question in its own favor.

The problems that the Ottoman Empire faced after the Crimean War were a sign that the empire's end was near. Although the Ottoman Empire did not enter war again until 1877, revolts and severe conflicts in different parts of the empire and excessive loans which bankrupted the empire's economy brought it to the verge of collapse. The conflict between Muslims and Christians in Jeddah (1858) and in Lebanon (1860-1861) which were provoked by the French and British, led to foreign intervention that resulted in the establishment of a privileged administration in these states. Walachia and Bogdan united to form the principality of Romania in 1861, the rebellions in Crete backed by Greece marked the beginning of the island's departure from the Ottoman Empire. Russia built a foreign policy based on Pan Slavism which called for the solidarity of all Slavic and Orthodox nations under Russian leadership. This policy provoked a rebellion in Herzegovina in 1875, then in Bulgaria in 1876. This was followed by Serbia and Montenegro declaring war. The Ottoman response towards the rebellion in Bulgaria was propagandized in Europe as a "Turkish atrocity", and this created anti-Turkish feelings among the British public that served Russia's purpose.

## The First Constitutional Era (1876 - 1908)

The Turkish public was filled with fury at the killings and expulsions of many Turks in the Balkans during the period of nationalist rebellions. In the middle of these events, Sultan Abdulaziz (1861-1866) was deposed by his ministers on May 30, 1876. He was succeeded by Murad V who was also deposed after three months, due to mental illness. Abdulhamid II (1876-1909) ascended to the throne and promised to establish a constitution. Abdulhamid II was the last Ottoman sultan who ruled with unchallenged power. Despite his deposition following the Young Turk Revolution of 1908, Abdulhamid II was credited by many Ottomans for delaying the unavoidable break-up of the Ottoman Empire for at least a few decades. He held the Ottoman Empire together with authoritarian methods and his cunning diplomatic maneuvers that played one European power against the other.

While the tension in the Balkans grew, the European powers held a conference in Istanbul in order to give autonomous status to Bosnia-Herzegovina and Bulgaria. In order to neutralize the effects of the conference, Abdulhamid II proclaimed a constitution. European powers at the conference rejected the constitution as insignificant. Russia continued to mobilize for war, which was declared on April 24, 1877. At the start of the war Russia destroyed all vessels along the Danube, and then marched towards Bulgaria. When they reached Pleven, Osman Pasha organized a brilliant defense and repelled two Russian attacks with huge casualties on the Russian side. Yet the heroic defense of Pleven eventually failed, and this allowed the

Russians to march towards Istanbul. Although Russia accepted the truce offered by Turkey in January 1878, it continued to move towards Istanbul. On the way they killed thousands of children, women, and old Turkish people with the co-operation of Bulgarian gangs. In the wake of these atrocities many Turks began to migrate from the Balkans towards Istanbul and Anatolia. Russia then agreed to a settlement with the Treaty of San Stefano (Ayastefanos) on March 3, 1878. According to this treat the Ottoman Empire would recognize the independence of Romania, Serbia and Montenegro, also the autonomy of Bulgaria. Alarmed by the extension of Russian power into the Balkans, the Great Powers later forced modifications of the treaty in the Congress of Berlin. The main modification made in Berlin was the dividing Bulgaria, according to earlier agreements among the Great Powers, to preclude the creation of a large new Slavic state. The northern and eastern parts of Bulgaria became separate principalities with different governors as they had been before (the Principality of Bulgaria and Eastern Rumelia). The Congress of Berlin also returned the region of Macedonia (originally part of Bulgaria under the San Stefano Treaty) to direct Ottoman administration. The Treaty of Berlin also suggested some reforms in favor of the Ottoman Armenian subject.

With the Treaty of Berlin, the Great Powers realized that the Ottoman Empire was so weak that it could not defend itself against the independence movements that were developing within its borders. The Great Powers then ceased to respect the territorial integrity of the Ottoman Empire. Great Britain settled in Cyprus in 1878 and temporarily occupied Egypt in 1882. France occupied Tunisia in 1881. Eastern Rumelia united with Bulgaria in 1885. The rebellion in Crete provoked by Greece led to a war with Greece which resulted in Turkish victory in 1897, but an autonomous administration was established there as the result of British and Russian intervention.

Apart from these losses, financial embarrassments forced Abdulhamid II to consent to foreign control over the national debt. In a decree issued in December 1881, a large portion of the empire's revenues were handed over to the Public Debt Administration for the benefit of mostly foreign bondholders. After Great Britain had a common cause against the Ottoman Empire with the other members of the Triple Entente (France and Russia) after the Treaty of Berlin, Abdulhamid approached

Germany as a possible friend of the empire. Kaiser Wilhelm II was twice hosted by Abdulhamid in Istanbul; first on October 21, 1889, and nine years later on October 5, 1898. German officers such as Baron von der Goltz were employed to oversee the reorganization of the Ottoman army. German government officials were brought in to reorganize the Ottoman government's finances. In 1899 the highly coveted the Baghdad Railway was given to the Germans. This was a part of Abdulhamid's foreign policy, which tried to play one power against another. The Kaiser's desire to extend German influence over the Middle East resulted in a strong German influence over the Porte.

## The Emergence of the Armenian Question

The Treaty of Berlin brought the Armenian question onto the Great Powers' agenda. The fact that it might lead to the dismemberment of Anatolian territory made it a matter of great importance to Russia and Britain, who held rival interests in the Middle East. Russia needed the collaboration of the Armenians in order to reach the Eastern Mediterranean and Mesopotamia. Great Britain needed the Armenians in order to prevent Russian expansion to the south. The Armenian question emerged as Armenians began to conduct terrorist activities in eastern Anatolia under the provocations of Russia and Great Britain. These provocations were made on the pretext of the reforms suggested in the Treaty of Berlin.

Armenian, Turkish and Muslim communities in the Ottoman Empire had been living together in a very peacefully until the imperialist powers began to show interest in the region. With the intervention of the imperialist powers came a mushrooming of Armenian political and social organizations. Indeed, beginning in the 1860s, local Armenian organizations were founded in Adana, Van, and Mush. These organizations united in 1880 to form the United Armenian Organizations. In the 1880s some more revolutionary Armenian organizations were established as well, such as the Black Cross, the Armenian societies in Van, and the National Guards in Erzurum.

Perceiving that they would be more influential abroad with the active and direct support of the Great Powers, Armenian nationalists decided to center their organizations outside Ottoman territory. They established the *Hinchak* Committee in Geneva in 1887, and the *Dashnak* Committee in Tbilisi in 1890.

Both of these Committees declared their basic goal to be the 'liberation from Ottoman rule of the territories of Eastern Anatolia and the Ottoman Armenians'. Armenian riots began soon after the establishment of these two effective political institutions.

In the twenty years between 1889 and 1909 there were almost 40 Armenian rebellions or terrorist activities. They involved many violent events in Istanbul. They attempted to assassinate Sultan Abdulhamid in 1905. The sultan was saved by chance. The measures taken by the Porte led to the Great Powers intervention. The Armenian question became more dangerous during the First World War.

## The Restoration of the Constitution in 1908

An opposition to Abdulhamid had started when he suspended the constitution in May 1878. In the first years of the twentieth century this opposition began to grow. One of his most severe opponents was the *Ittihad ve Terakki Cemiyeti* (the Committee of Union and Progress- *CUP*). The CUP was one of the Jön Türk (Young Turks) organizations that wanted to restore the constitutional monarchy. The *CUP* became popular among military officers, whose participation made the movement much stronger. Thus the opponents of the *CUP* abroad moved into the Ottoman Empire. In the middle of 1908, the Thessalonica branch of the *CUP* prepared a revolt in response to the effects of the Macedonian question. They believed that reforming the Balkans was the only way to prevent them from leaving the Ottoman Empire. When the *CUP* revolted in Thessalonica in order to restore the constitution, the sultan's attempt to suppress this uprising failed due to the popularity of the movement among the troops themselves. Rebellion spread rapidly. Abdulhamid announced the restoration of the constitution on July 23, 1908. On April 13, 1909 a counter-revolt against the constitutional monarchy broke out in Istanbul. This counter-revolt was suppressed by the Movement Army (*Hareket Ordusu*). Abdulhamid was accused of supporting the counter-revolt, and he was deposed. He was succeeded by his brother, Mehmed Reshad (Mehmed VI). Mehmed VI held the position of sultan from 1909 to 1918, but was in fact an impotent leader. After the restoration of the constitution the CUP became an influential political party with a majority in parliament from 1908 to 1913. In spite of parliamentary elections, non-partisan figures from the pre-revolutionary period still dominated the Ottoman cabinet. These non-partisan figures became targets of the CUP. On January 23, 1913 the CUP came to power through a coup called *Bab-ı Ali Baskını*. The CUP and its leaders Enver, Cemal and Talat Pashas held power during the final years of the Ottoman Empire.

The constitutional monarchy did not prevent the dismemberment of the Ottoman Empire as the Young Turks and the CUP had claimed. Soon after the restoration of the constitution, Austria annexed Bosnia-Herzegovina on October 5, 1908. The next day Bulgaria declared its independence. Greece annexed Crete on May 9, 1910. Taking advantage of the situation, on September 29, 1911 Italy invaded Tripolitania (known today as Libya) with the support of the Great Powers. With local backing, Turkish troops under the command of Mustafa Kemal and Enver Pashas successfully fought back the Italians for about a year. Italy then occupied the Dodecanese islands in order to break through the Turkish resistance. The Ottomans eventually signed the Treaty of Ouchy (Ushi) with Italy on October 15, 1912. The Ottomans were forced to sign this treaty not because of Italian military successes, but because t he more important Balkan War had just begun and urgently demanded their full attention. Treaty of Ouchy gave Italy possession of Tripolitania and the Dodecanese islands.

## The Balkan Wars (1912 - 1913)

While the Ottomans were occupied with Tripolitania, Russia brought a final end to Ottoman power in the Balkans. For many years Russia had been provoking Balkan states to rebel against Ottoman authority. In the spring of 1912 various Christian Balkan nations formed a network of military alliances known as the Balkan League. In late September, both the League and the Ottoman Empire mobilized their armies. After issuing an impossible ultimatum to the Porte, Montenegro declared war on the Ottoman Empire in October 1913. Three other Balkan nations soon followed Montenegro's example. Ottoman forces were defeated by the Balkan League. The basic reason of the defeat was political dissidence inside the army. The Bulgarian forces advanced up to the Çatalca, a district of Istanbul. Greece seized Thessalonica, and Serbia sized Bitola (Manastır). Then a peace conference was held in London on November 29, 1913. The Porte wanted the Great Powers to mediate. The Great

Powers acknowledged the independence of Albania on December 17, 1913. They even forced the Ottoman Empire to cede Rumelia, including eastern Thrace, and the Aegean Islands to the Balkan states. During this time, the Union and Progress party took power in the Ottoman Empire with a coup on January 23, 1913. At the end of the Conference, Bulgaria received the northern portion of Thrace between Enos on the Aegean Sea and Midia on the Black Sea. This was a great loss for the Ottoman Empire and created ill-feelings among the Turkish people.

As a result of the terms of the Treaty of London, the Second Balkan War broke out between the combatants in June 1913 because of Bulgaria's tremendous gains. A final peace was agreed upon at the Treaty of Bucharest on August 12, 1913. With successive treaties with Bulgaria and Greece, the Ottomans restored much of its losses from the First Balkan War. Today's borders between the Turkish Republic and Bulgaria and Greece were drawn at this time.

The Balkan Wars were one of the most severe catastrophes that the Turks had faced in their whole history. Five centuries of Turkish hegemony in Rumelia came to an end except for Eastern Thrace. Thousands of Turks in Rumelia were exposed to atrocities. Most of them left their possession and were forced to migrate to Anatolia. The migration left the Ottomans in a very difficult position as they had already experienced great economic strain. The Turks who still live in the Balkans continue to experience economic and social discrimination.

## D. Dissolution (1914 - 1922)

### The First World War: The Last War of the Ottoman Empire

On June 28, 1914, the Archduke Franz Ferdinand was killed by a Bosnian Serb student in Sarajevo. The Archduke Ferdinand had been the heir to the throne of the Austro-Hungarian Empire. His assassin was a member of the Young Bosnia organization, whose aims included the unification of the southern Slavs and independence from the Austro-Hungarian Empire. The assassination in Sarajevo set in motion a series of fast-moving events that escalated into a full-scale war. Austria-Hungary declared war on Serbia under the pretext that Serbia had deliberately failed to punish those responsible for the assassination. The major European powers were at war within a matter of weeks because of overlapping agreements for collective defense and the complex nature of international alliances. The conflict, however, also had more complex causes.

The Allied Powers (France, Britain, and Russia) were quickly pulled into war when Germany (the leading state of the Central Powers) declared war on Russia on August 1, 1914. Germany was an emerging world power that had begun to covet Great Britain's overseas possessions. To defend itself against German ambitions, Britain had formed a common cause in the international arena with Russia. This meant that Britain consented to Russia's historic aims in the Balkans and the Turkish Straits in exchange for Russian acknowledgment of its strategic interests in the Middle East. The alliance between Britain and Russia severely threatened the territorial integrity of the Ottoman Empire. Despite all this, the Ottoman Empire's position at the initial phase of the war was very ambiguous. Despite the Ottoman Empire's alliance with Germany dating from the Treaty of Berlin in 1817, the leading cadres of the Union and Progress Party which had held power since 1913 (Enver, Cemal and Talat Pashas) sought an alliance with Britain to fend off Russian pressure. The Union and Progress Party's leaders also found Germany's interests in Ottoman lands be to too excessive. Neither Great Britain nor France however, accepted the Ottoman offer for an alliance. Talat Pasha even sought an alliance with Russia, but failed. The Ottoman government believed that the Allied powers had already agreed on dividing up the Ottoman Empire in a major war. Therefore, the Union and Progress Party (whose supporters sympathized with the Germans) allied itself with Wilhelm II on August 2, 1914. It is interesting to note that in 1911 the Ottoman government had ordered two warships from Britain (the *Sultan Osman* and the *Reshadiye*). The Ottoman government had collected donations from its people to pay for these warships. Yet Britain, who had deliberately delayed their delivery, seized the warships on August 3. It was clear that Britain did not want these warships to be used against it.

## Ottoman Entry in the First World War

As a matter of fact, neither the Ottoman Assembly nor the majority of the people wanted to go war. The leaders of the governing party however, were eager to side with the Central powers in belief that they might prevent the empire from being dismembered by the Allied powers. The incident that led the Ottoman Empire to enter the First World War was the giving of refuge to the 19,000 ton German battle cruiser *Goeben* and the 5,000 ton light cruiser *Breslau*. The Ottoman government declared that these ships had been bought, and renamed them *Yavuz* and *Midilli*, respectively. The Ottoman Government might have thought that these ships were replacements for the *Sultan Osman* and the *Reshadiye*. Shortly thereafter, the Russian ports of Sevastopol and Odessa were bombarded on October 29, 1914 with these warships under the command of Admiral Souchon - without the authorization of the Ottoman Parliament or cabinet. This was a provocation planned by the Germans in order to bring the Ottoman state into the war. Ottoman entry in the war would lighten the Allied pressure on the Western and Eastern fronts, where German (and Austro-Hungarian) forces had begun to suffer serious setbacks at Marne and Galicia. After this incident, Russia declared war against the Ottoman Empire on 3 November, and Britain and France on 5 November. Thus, the Ottomans found themselves in the war. The Ottoman Sultan called for a jihad, holy war, on 23 November to all Muslims, including those who were living in Russia, Britain and France. This was what the Germans wanted, as Britain with its Muslim subjects in its colonies (particularly in India) might have experienced great difficulty if Muslims revolted against them. This was valid for Russia as well, who had a large Muslim population to be worried about.

The Turkish army fought in different fronts at the same time: Caucasia, Iraq, the Dardanelles, Egypt, Yemen, and Macedonia. At the beginning of the war, Turkish troops were ordered by their commander-in-chief Enver Pasha to march to Caucasia in order to encircle Russian troops. But as the result of ill-made plans, nearly 90 thousand Turkish soldiers died. The reason for the losses were mostly ignorance of winter conditions, a freezing winter, lack of clothing, starvation and disease when they climbed Allahu Ekber Mountain on the way to meet Russian troops. In the end, Russian troops invaded Manzikert, Van, Erzincan, Erzurum, and Trabzon by February 1916. Thereafter the Armenians living in the region began to revolt against the Ottoman Empire and carried out systematic massacres against the Turkish and Muslim population there with the encouragement of Russia. It is clear from the archival and civilian sources that the Ottoman Armenian subjects in reasonable numbers collaborated and were involved in activities to facilitate the enemy's invasion.

## The Armenian Question in 1915

The Ottoman government - against numerous rebellions begun after 1890 promptly following Armenian massacres which resulted in the murder of tens of thousands of Turks - informed the most important persons of the Armenian congregation and the Armenian deputies that the "Government will take necessary precautions if Armenians continue to stab Turks in the back and assassinate them". For the Ottomans government it became necessary to guarantee security behind its own borders as it was engaging in war on various fronts. The events did not stop but increased, and assaults towards defenseless Turkish women and children increased. Therefore, the Ottoman government decided to immigrate (*tehcir* in the Ottoman language) the Armenians who were involved in the uprising to a safer place, namely Syria and Lebanon which were a part of the Ottoman Empire. It is important to point out that the Arabic originated word *tehcir* means "immigration", it definitely does not mean "deportation" or "exile". Hence the law commonly known as the *Tehcir Law* is the same as the "Temporary Law of the Military Measures to be Taken for Those Who Resist the Governmental Acts and Supplementations." The protection of the lives and properties of Armenians following the process of immigration, and provision of their needs such as food, drink and rest were left to the regional authorities along the transfer route. It was decreed that the immigrating Armenians be allowed to carry along all of their belongings, and arrangements regarding their established properties were to be prepared and submitted to the authorities concerned.

It was an unpleasant, but inevitable military measure taken by the Ottoman government who was in a major war. No power in the world could have remained unmoved when faced with a similar situation. The emigration was also taken as the result of an insistent suggestion made by the German General Chief of Staff. Indeed, one of the reasons of the immigration was to prevent the conflict between Armenian and Turkish people in Eastern Anatolia, as Armenian assault provoked Turkish reaction. It should not be forgotten that the *Tehcir Law* was issued when the Turkish troops were struggling at the Battle of the Dardanelles, one of the severe battles of the Turks in the major war. The immigration process was carried out in a successful way as most of the Armenians were transferred safely to Syria. Of course, some local authorities acted in an irresponsible way and some gangs attacked Armenians troops for revenge while they were immigrating.

It is hardly possible to call this event the "genocide" that Armenians claim. It is true that what happened in 1915 was a very sad story for the Armenians. One should not forget the suffering of the Turks and other Muslim populations in Anatolia as the result of Armenian assaults. In this sense, the Turks and Armenians killed each other in a reciprocal fight.

There is another point that is always missing: the two nations had been peacefully living together for centuries under Ottoman rule until the middle of the nineteenth century. Whenever the Great powers showed interests in the region, the nature of the relations between the Armenians and Turks dramatically changed. If one needs to put blame somewhere it should be the imperial western powers, neither the Turks nor the Armenians.

If we look at the present position of Turkish-Armenian relations, there are certain and perpetual obstacles for the reconciliation and comprehension of the problem. The first one is the political issue. This one mostly comes from the Armenian Diaspora trying to force politicians of different countries, who are actually more concerned with their home politics and their voters than with the Armenian genocide, to pass resolutions against Turkey. This has done nothing other than make the issue political and widens the gap between the parties for reconciliation. More importantly this process paves the way for a liquidation of history. The passing of resolutions respecting the so-called Armenian genocide in some third-party countries' parliaments does not constitute a historical proof of the so-called Armenian genocide. It makes the issue a more complicated and political one. In return for these activities, Turkey uses its political, economic, and diplomatic power to evade the impact of these political activities.

## The Battle of Dardanelles or the Dardanelles Campaign

One of the major battles in the war took place at Gallipoli (known as the Battle of Çanakkale in Turkish, Gallipoli or the Dardanelles Campaign in Britain, France, Australia, and New

Zealand). A joint British and French operation was mounted in an effort to eventually capture the Ottoman capital of Istanbul.

The reason of the battle is that the Allies struggled throughout the war to open an effective supply route to Russia who had been struggling against the uprising led by Lenin. The German Empire and Austria-Hungary blocked Russia's land trade routes to Europe, and no easy sea route existed. The Black Sea's only entrance was through the Dardanelles and the Bosporus, which was controlled by the Ottoman Empire.

First Lord of the Admiralty, Winston Churchill of the United Kingdom, put forward his first plans for a naval attack on the Dardanelles. A plan for an attack and invasion of the Gallipoli peninsula was eventually approved by the British cabinet in January 1915.

The Allies' first major naval attack was launched on the Dardanelles on March 18, 1915. A massive fleet under the command of Admiral de Robeck containing no fewer than 16 battleships tried to advance through the Dardanelles. Yet almost every ship was damaged by sea mines which were laid along the Asian shore by the Turkish minelayer Nusret. Trawlermen had been used by the British as minesweepers. The Allies retreated as the Turks opened fire on them, leaving the minefields intact. Then three battleships were sunk by the Turkish artillery: the British ships *Ocean* and *Irresistible*, and the French ship *Bouvet*. The British battle cruiser *Inflexible* and the French battleships *Suffren* and *Gaulois* were badly damaged.

These losses prompted the Allies to cease any further attempts to force the straits by naval power alone. The defeat of the British fleet had also given the Turkish troops a morale boost. After the failure of the naval attacks, it was decided that ground forces were necessary to eliminate the Turkish mobile artillery.

In early 1915, Australian and New Zealand volunteer soldiers were encamped in Egypt. The infantry was formed into the Australian and New Zealand Army Corps (*ANZAC*). General Hamilton also had the regular British 29th and 10th Divisions and the French Oriental Expeditionary Corps. The allied forces began invading the Gallipoli Peninsula on April 25, 1915. However, they met unimaginable Turkish resistance. At the beginning Turkish troops could not hold the invader's advance, but they could not advance as planned (they advanced just three kilometers in three months). Then on the sixth of August two

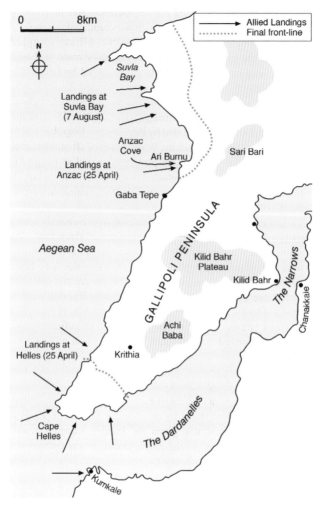

Allied infantry divisions landed at Suvla. Once again the Turks, under the command of lieutenant colonel Mustafa Kemal, were able to win the race for the high grounds of the Anafarta Hills, thereby rendering the Suvla front another case of static trench warfare. The battle lasted until the end of December without any great Allied successes. Ironically the evacuation which started in December was the greatest Allied success of the campaign. The last Allied troops departed from Gallipoli at the end of the first week of January 1916. In the end, Turkish casualties were about 250 thousand, and the Allies' casualties amounted to nearly 150 thousand.

The battle of the Dardanelles is one of the finest and bravest moments in the history of the Turkish people. It was a final surge in the defense of the motherland as the centuries-old Ottoman Empire was crumbling; which laid the grounds for the Turkish National Struggle and the foundation of the new Turkish Republic eight years later, led by Atatürk, a commander in Gallipoli himself. Even to this day, *ANZAC* Day is commemorated in Australia and New Zealand, and it is considered that the battle marked the birth of the collective national identities of both those nations, replacing that of the collective identity of the British Empire.

Turks had bravely resisted and defeated the gigantic allies' navies and armies at Gallipoli. However, the situation on the Egyptian front was not going smoothly. The aim of this campaign, which was encouraged by the Germans, was to re-establish Ottoman control over Egypt and particularly the Suez in which the British Empire route to India would be cut off. It was a failure.

### Secret Agreements

Sharif Hussein bin Ali, Emir of Hedjaz, rebelled against Ottoman rule in 1916 during the Arab revolt. His aim was to establish a single unified independent Arab state spanning from Aleppo in Syria to Aden in Yemen. This was a British promise in return for his revolt against the Ottoman Empire. As a matter of fact, this was a part of the Great Powers' policy of partitioning the Ottoman Empire. Great Britain and the France made a secret agreement, called The Sykes-Picot Agreement of May 1916. This Agreement defined their respective spheres of post-World War I influence and control in the Middle East, after the expected downfall of the Ottoman Empire. Accordingly, Britain was allocated mandate control of the areas roughly comprising Jordan, Iraq and a small area around Haifa, to allow access to a Mediterranean port. France was allocated mandate control of south-eastern Anatolia.

The agreement was later expanded to include Italy and Russia. Russia was to receive Eastern Anatolia, while the Italians would get the Aegean islands and a sphere of influence around Izmir in southwest Anatolia. This was not all. Britain also supported Zionist plans for a Jewish "national home" in Palestine with the Balfour Declaration of 1917 as part of the partition plan of the Ottoman Empire.

The Russian Revolution of 1917 led to Russia being denied its claims in the Ottoman Empire. At the same time Lenin released a copy of the confidential Sykes-Picot Agreement as well as other treaties causing great embarrassment among the allies and growing distrust among the Arabs. The Russian Revolution also led to withdraw of Russian troops from where they invaded the Ottoman lands by signing the Brest-Litovski Agreement of March 1918. However, the military position of Turkish troops in Iraq and Syria was getting worse. The other members of the Central Powers withdrew from the war by accepting defeat. Therefore, trusting Wilson's principles which suggested that the Turkish portion of the present Ottoman Empire should have its sovereignty secured, the Ottoman government decided to offer a truce to the Allies and signed the Mudros Armistice on October 30, 1918.

The Ottoman Empire which covered the entire Balkans, most of the Middle East and North Africa as well as Caucasia, succeeded in forming relatively stability at the height of its power during the sixteenth and seventeenth centuries and most of the eighteenth century. This period was called Pax-Ottomana (Ottoman Peace) by some Ottoman historians. The term is meaningful if one compares the regions that experienced social, economic, and political instability following the demise of Ottoman rule and especially after the end of the Cold War.

## The Mudros Armistice

The Armistice which ended the hostilities between the Ottoman Empire and the Allies was signed by the Minister of Marine Affairs, Rauf Bey and British Admiral Calthorpe aboard the *HMS Agamemnon* in the Mudros port on the island of Lemnos, marking the defeat of the Ottoman Empire in World War I. Before the Armistice was signed Amiral Calthorpe had guaranteed Rauf Bey that Istanbul would not be occupied and that Greek warships would not be brought to Istanbul. With its 25 items, the Armistice suggested in sum that the Ottomans had to renounce all of their empire, with the exception of Anatolia and give up all their garrisons in Hedjaz, Yemen, Syria, Iraq, Tripolitania, and Cyrenaica. The allies occupied the area around the straits of the Dardanelles and the Bosporus, and the tunnels of the Taurus Mountains. The Allies also had the right to occupy six provinces with Armenian populations in north-eastern Anatolia in case of disorder, as well as any strategic point which mattered to the security of the Allies. The Allies' first goal was to control all munitions and their distribution. The second goal was to disband the various small army units, by either combining them into bigger and more controllable units, or sending them home.

If one carefully examines the items of the Armistice, it can be seen that the Allies' aim was to open Anatolia for invasion without meeting any serious resistance. Without waiting for the peace conference that should have been held after the war, the Allies began to invade Anatolia under various pretexts. First, Britain unlawfully invaded Mosul just three days after the armistice signed. When the Armistice was signed the British troops were located 60 kilometers south of Mosul province. They should not have moved forward to the north according to the armistice terms.

In contradiction of earlier promises, 73 units of British, French, Italian and Greek warships anchored in Istanbul on November 12, 1918. The Turkish provinces of Adana, and Mersin in southern Anatolia were invaded by the French in December 1918; Antep was invaded by the British on December 17, 1918, as was Marash on February 22, and Ufra on March 24, 1919. Antalya, Fethiye, Bodrum, and Konya were invaded by Italians. Furthermore, Britain took the Black Sea regions of Samsun and Merzifon under its control. Britain turned Antep and Marash over to the French, while they showed much interested in Iraq, the oil rich area.

# CHAPTER 11

## Turkish National Struggle (1919 - 1923)

It should be noted that the Turkish National Struggle was the consequence of the political and military developments that occurred between 1919 and 1922 which were materialized under the Mudros Armistice conditions. However, this struggle has another aspect in the sense that it accelerated the Turkish modernization process which had begun since the eighteenth century. At the end of the Turkish National Struggle its leader, Mustafa Kemal Atatürk, founded the Turkish Republic. This is important in Turkish history because it marks the first time that sovereignty was passed directly to the people.

The Armistice of Mudros virtually put an end to the Ottoman Empire as its lands other than Anatolia and Eastern Thrace were surrendered to the Allies. When the leading officers of the Ottoman Army, such as Mustafa Kemal, Kazim Karabekir and others returned from their posts to Istanbul in November 1918, they found the capital city virtually occupied. There is a famous quote from Mustafa Kemal when he saw the enemy warships anchored in the Bosporus: "they (the enemies) will return as they have come." This symbolized his determination to resistance against the invasion.

The Ottoman government and the sultan were too weak to enforce their own decisions or restore law and order in many areas, mostly because the capital city was occupied by the Allies. Much worse was that most members of the Ottoman government did not see any solution other than co-operation with the invaders, whose intention has already been stated above. Therefore, since the country was in a state of collapse and the Istanbul government had no vision to overcome the situation that the empire found itself in, a series of meetings were held between Mustafa Kemal and his colleagues in Istanbul regarding the future of the country. There were conflicting factions with conflicting visions, but what united the various factions was the view that the Allies' goal was the elimination of sovereignty in their homeland. This perception was the driving force binding the mainly Turkish inhabitants of Anatolia to unite. It was concluded that as the Istanbul government and the sultan himself were under foreign control, the only way to escape from foreign domination was to go to Anatolia in order to organize a national movement against the occupations. It was a great change for the nationalists when some colleagues of Mustafa Kemal such as Refet Bele, Kazim Karabekir, and Ali Fuad Cebesoy, etc. were appointed to army corps in different parts of Anatolia by the Ministry of Defense (Harbiye Naziri), which consisted of mostly nationalist officers.

Meanwhile, the Allied governments were about to reach a decision on the future of Western Anatolia. Izmir and western Anatolia had been given to the Italians in the secret agreement to divide Anatolia made among the Allies during the war. However, when Britain brought the possibility of a Greek invasion of Izmir onto the table, Italy left the Peace Conference on April 24, 1919 and did not return until May 5th. In the absence of Italy, Lloyd George persuaded France and the United States to favor Greece's interest over Italy's in Izmir and western Anatolia. It can easily be said that the Greek invasion of Izmir on May 15, 1919 aroused national feelings and accelerated people's joining in the Movements of National Struggle by organizing the local Society to Defend Right and Interest (*Müdafa-i Hukuk Cemiyetleri*) and by establishing local Militia Forces (*Kuvay-i Milliye*) in order to defend thei r regions against the invaders.

At this time, Mustafa Kemal had the opportunity of having an official position to go to Anatolia when Admiral Calthorpe, the British Commissioner in the Ottoman Empire, gave a memorandum to the government alleging that the Greeks in the Black Sea region were subject to Turkish civilian assaults. Then the tone of the memorandum became threatening: "If this was not stopped, Allied intervention would be inevitable". As a matter of fact, though the real threat existed for the Turks who were under attack by some Greek gangs who were encouraged by the Allied powers, this was an excuse for giving way to Allied intervention. In order to avoid further foreign intervention, the Sultan Mehmed Vahdeddin (Mehmed VI, 1918-1922), the 36th and the last Ottoman sultan appointed Mustafa Kemal as an Inspector General of the ninth army on April 30, 1919 with wide power. The official duty of Mustafa Kemal was t o disarm the Turkish army and to restore the situation there; in this sense, he would inspect the progress of the application of the Armistice terms. However, this duty disguised Mustafa Kemal's main goal of organizing a national resistance movement. Therefore, it can be easily seen that Mustafa Kemal had two main objectives: the first was to struggle against the foreign invasion; the second was to struggle for the establishment of national sovereignty, which meant struggling against the sultan and the Ottoman government. The name of Mustafa Kemal was familiar to the Turkish people as his success at the Battle of Gallipoli gave him some credentials.

## The National Awakening

Mustafa Kemal left Istanbul on a passenger cargo vessel, the Bandirma, on the evening of May 16, 1919. He was headed for Samsun, a district in the middle of the Black Sea region, where he stepped ashore on May 19, 1919. This date is accepted as the beginning of the National Struggle Movement. He made the people of Samsun aware of the Greek landings and foreign invasion of the country. He also stated that the Istanbul government could do nothing about the invasion.

Mustafa Kemal informed his colleagues by telegraph that he was in Samsun and soon would advance into inner Anatolia. His final destination was Sivas, which was much safer than any other place in order to organize the national resistance movement. Sivas was also chosen because his close friend Kazim Karabekir's army corps was in Erzurum, not very far away from there. Also, Sivas was away from the Istanbul government's influence.

To reach Sivas, he moved to Havza where he formed links with various nationalist groups and called the people for mass meetings. He sent telegrams of protest to foreign embassies and to the War Ministry in Istanbul about British reinforcements in the area and about British aid to Greek brigand gangs. While officially occupied with the disarming of the military, he had increased his various contacts in order to build his movement's momentum. Then he moved to Amasya where he met Rauf Bey, Ali Fuat Bey, and Refet Bey. After some preparatory work they issued a document on June 22, 1919 called the "Amasya Circular" which called the Turkish people's attention to the foreign attacks which threatened their existence. Distributed across Anatolia, the circular declared Turkey's independence and integrity to be in danger. It also called for a national conference to be held in Sivas, and before that, for a preparatory congress comprising representatives from the eastern provinces of Anatolia to be held in Erzurum.

According to the Istanbul government, Mustafa Kemal had

gone too far by issuing the circular. The sultan recalled him to Istanbul from Erzurum on the night of July 7, 1919. There was no other choice for Mustafa Kemal but to resign from all his official posts, and he did so. His leadership in the national movement however, remained intact. He and others continued their work for the Erzurum Congress, which was held from July $23^{rd}$ to August $7^{th}$. This was the second step in the founding of national unity.

Meanwhile, the Greek invasion raised a national awakening in western Anatolia where some congresses were also held. Delegates from western Anatolia were sent to the Congress of Sivas held on September 4 to 11, 1919. The Congress of Sivas made a number of decisions that fundamentally shaped the future policy of the national movements. It was decided to recognize Turkey's boundaries as established in the Mudros Armistice, and to rename the local organizations "The Society to Defend the Rights and Interests of the Provinces of Anatolia and Rumeli". It was also agreed at Sivas that the parliament should meet in Istanbul, even if it was obvious that this parliament could not function under the occupation. It was a great chance to build the base and legitimacy of the national movement. There was another important decision made at the congress that formalized a "Representative Committee" that would handle the distribution and implementation of the Congress's decisions. This could easily be turned into a new government if the Allies decided to disband the whole Ottoman governing structure. Mustafa Kemal was elected as leader of the Committee. Therefore, with the Sivas Congress, the movement of Anatolia led by Mustafa Kemal, became an organized movement that covered almost the whole country. The Representative Committee acted like a government as it appointed Ali Fuad Pasha as the commander of the Western Anatolian Nationalist Militia Forces in order to fight against the Greek army.

The National Movement in Anatolia became so effective that the Istanbul government was constrained to pay attention to the nationalists. Therefore, Prime Minister Damat Ferid Pasha, a bitter opponent of the National Movement and feverishly pro-British, had to resign and was replaced by Ali Riza Pasha, who had sympathy for the nationalists. Ali Riza Pasha sent navy minister Salih Pasha to negotiate with Mustafa Kemal. The two met in Amasya on 20-22 October 1919 and signed a protocol in which Salih Pasha and Mustafa Kemal agreed that Turkish territorial integrity would be defended as the Mudros Armistice suggested. Salih Pasha also agreed that the Ottoman Parliament would be assembled somewhere in Anatolia, not in Istanbul. On December 27$^{th}$, Mustafa Kemal and his Representative Committee moved to Ankara to establish an enduring center of the National Movements. Another point is that Ankara was much closer to the western front and also to Istanbul. Thus Mustafa Kemal would be in a position to extend his control over the Parliament via his followers who were selected as members of Parliament from Anatolia. Ankara also held a strategic importance for Mustafa Kemal and his Representative Committee.

## The National Oath

Due to British pressure, Ali Riza Pasha could not recognize many of the terms of the Amasya Protocol. He was however, able to assemble the Ottoman Parliament in Istanbul on January 12, 1920. Before that, new elections were held for the Ottoman parliament. Ali Riza's government might have been seen as a chance for the Nationalists. The house of parliament however, was under the shadow of the British battalion stationed in Istanbul. The parliament accepted the National Oath on January 28, 1920 as Mustafa Kemal had suggested to the MPs who had visited him before going to Istanbul.

The first clause of the Oath was important: The future of the territories inhabited by an Arab majority at the time of the signing of the Mudros Treaty on October 30, 1918 would be determined by a referendum. The territories which were not occupied at that time and inhabited by a Turkish-Muslim majority were to be the homeland of the Turkish nation. The other clause of the National Oath suggested that in order to develop in every field, the country should be independent and free; all restrictions on political, judicial and financial development would be removed.

The leaders of the Turkish Nationalist Movement formulated their objectives in the National Oath, in which they determined to continue the resistance for the salvation and complete independence of the Turkish nation. It limited the boundaries of a new Turkey inhabited by a Muslim majority, united in religion, culture and race.

The Allied powers were obviously not delighted with the declaration of the National Oath. They showed their reaction by officially invading Istanbul on March 16, 1920. The Ottoman Parliament was dissolved on the 11th of April by the Sultan. The MPs who were arrested by the British were sent to Malta. Others who escaped from arrest took refuge with Mustafa Kemal in Ankara. Mustafa Kemal had wanted the Parliament to assemble in Ankara or somewhere in Anatolia like Bursa, as he guessed the end result.

## Rebirth of a Nation

Mustafa Kemal sent a memorandum to the Allied representatives in Istanbul and to the French, British, and Italian parliaments to protest the invasion. Kazim Karabekir, the Commander of the fifteenth army corps, arrested British Colonel Rawlinson along with 20 other British subjects to protest the invasion of Istanbul. After that, Mustafa Kemal forbade any kind of relationship with the Istanbul government. He issued a circular on March 19th stating that a new parliament should be gathered with extraordinary power in Ankara. The parliament would be composed of deputies of the old parliament who would come to Ankara and by new members to be elected by the Turkish people. At this point the question was whether the Parliament would be a continuance of the Ottoman Parliament or not. Mustafa Kemal wanted this Parliament to be a "constitutional" one. However, in order to escape a long discussion of its nature, he called it a Grand National Assembly (*GNA*). The *GNA* consisted of about 300 MPs and opened on April 23, 1920, with Mustafa Kemal selected as its chairman. It is quite obvious that the new formation in Anatolia was not only a movement against the invading powers, but also a formation of a new state. The *GNA* accepted the First Constitution on January 20, 1921. The First Constitution stated:

1 - National power concentrated in the National Assembly is the fundamental principle for the future of the country.

2 - The Grand National Assembly is vested with legislative and executive powers.

3 - A committee to be elected from within the Assembly will exercise executive power. The chairman of the Assembly will also preside over this committee.

Subsequent events following the opening of the *GNA* forced the new administration to choose between life and death. They had to struggle not only with Istanbul and the Allied powers but also with revolts in Anatolia, which were mostly provoked by the Allied powers. After the dissolution of the Ottoman Power, Ali Riza Pasha was replaced by the pro-British Damat Ferit Pasha, who was in co-operation with the Allied powers in order to put the Ankara government in a vulnerable position. In the meantime, an international conference was held in San Remo by the Allied powers on 18-26 April 1920 in order to discuss the terms of the Peace Treaty which would be signed with the Turks. The draft treaty that the Allied powers offered to the Turks at the Conference was unacceptable, as it called for the dismemberment of Turkey. On June 22nd, Greek forces invaded west of the line between Uşak and Bursa in order to push the Turks into accepting the Allies' peace offers. On July 8th, Greeks invaded Bursa, then the whole Aegean region, and then eastern Thrace.

Following these pressures, Damat Ferit Pasha's government signed the Treaty of Sevres on August 10, 1920. This treaty solidified the partitioning of the Ottoman Empire in accordance with secret agreements among the Allied powers. Turkey, whose boundaries were defined at the National Oath, was limited to Istanbul and its hinterland, and a small part of Anatolia. The Allied powers did not leave any space for the Turks to live in Anatolia. The Sevres Treaty was strongly rejected by the GNA and those who signed it were declared "traitors". It was an abortive agreement in the absence of the Ottoman parliament, which was forced to be abolished by the Allied invasion of Istanbul. In the absence of the Parliament, it was not sent to sultan Mehmed VI to be ratified, nor was it published in *Takvim-i Vakayi*, the official newspaper. Besides this, no country other than Greece ratified the treaty.

### Fighting For Freedom

The Treaty was not ratified because of the strong opposition of the *GNA* and the Turkish people. Yet this did not mean that the Allied powers abandoned their objectives in Turkey. They provoked some revolts in Anatolia with the collaboration of the Istanbul government. They also produced propaganda in eastern Anatolia calling for the establishment of autonomous Armenian and Kurdish states. Armenians, who were eager to have a share in eastern Anatolia for their Great Armenian project, which had been backed by the Great Powers for a long time, attacked and massacred the people in the region. Kazım Karabekir fended off the Armenian forces in eastern Anatolia. On November 18, 1920, the forces called a cease-fire and peace on the Eastern Front was achieved by the Gümrü Treaty, signed on December 3, 1920.

Another struggle which began just after the Mudros Armistice was on the southern front. Following the Armistice, the southeastern region of Turkey was occupied by French forces. The people in the region organized a great resistance movement with the support of the GNA against the French forces. The conflict with the French was ended by the Ankara Agreement of October 20, 1921.

Another conflict happened in eastern Thrace during the Greek invasion of 1920. Severe and great conflicts resulted from the Greek invasion on Turkey's western front. With the Greek occupation of Izmir, the people living in the occupied area organized militia forces in order to defend themselves against Greek cruelty in the region. The militias began to transform into an organized national Army after the opening of the Grand National Assembly. Thus, the *GNA* or the Ankara government had an organized national army by the end of 1920. This was a major step taken by the *GNA* because the Greeks began to campaign inside Anatolia by the beginning of 1921.

On January 6, 1921, the Greek invasion troops began to advance from Bursa and Uflak to Eskiflehir and Afyon, but they were defeated at the First Battle of ‹nönü on January 11, 1921 and retreated. After this first success by the Turks on the western front, the Allied Powers saw it necessary to make some alterations in the terms of the Sevres Treaty. Therefore, the Turks were invited by the Allied powers to a conference held in London between February 21 and March 12, 1921. Although the Turks could not make any important resolutions during the conference, it was very useful as it publicized the Turkish National Movements all over the world. As the *GNA* rejected the Allies' offer, Greek troops were encouraged by the British to mount a new attack, but they were defeated once again at ‹nönü on March 30th.

Meanwhile the Italians, who had recently developed good relationships with Ankara, began to withdraw from Antalya and its environs in June. This evidenced a break up among the Allies. Greek forces however, gained success in the Battles of Eskiflehir and Kütayha on June 10 - 24, 1921. Mustafa Kemal ordered the Turkish army to withdraw east of Sakarya, just 50 km away from Ankara, in order to take a defensive position. It was a tactical withdrawal to gain time to re-organize the army. This raised a number of critical questions in the GNA which was in a state of panic.

At this point, Mustafa Kemal got the GNA to convince him to take the command in his hand. Mustafa Kemal Pasha was given the position of Commander-in-Chief by the Grand National Assembly under a law accepted on August 5, 1921. He was preparing to take necessary measures for a final strike on the Greek troops in Anatolia. However, the Greek troops, who had won the last battle, hastened to attack Turkish troops in order to deal them a final defeat. However, at the end of the Battle of Sakarya, which was fought on a front extending about 100 kilometers, between August 23 and September 13, 1921, the Greek troops were forced to withdraw to the west of Sakarya and the Greek offensive in Anatolia ended. The *GNA*, who had criticized him before the battle, rewarded Mustafa Kemal on September 19, 1921 with the rank of Marshal and the title of Ghazi (Veteran) for his achievements in the Battle of Sakarya.

The achievements at Sakarya raised the GNA's credibility not only in the eyes of the Turkish people but also in the whole world, and even within the Allied powers. The GNA signed the Treaty of Ankara with France on October 20, 1921. Another agreement - the Treaty of Kars - was signed with the states of Azerbaijan, Georgia, and Armenia. Thus Turkey's eastern frontier became stable. After Sakarya, Greek-British co-operation also greatly ended.

After all these developments, Greece wanted the Allied forces to mediate for a truce with the Turks, but Ankara rejected it. Though the Turkish army had won a great victory, it was not yet in a position to drive out the invaders from Anatolia. They needed reasonable amount of time to make the troops ready for a final battle. It took almost a year for a final attack on the Greek army. During this time, some troops from the southern and eastern fronts transferred to the western front. Ammunitions were also transferred to the front. Mustafa Kemal, commander-in-chief, issued an order stating that all preparations had to be done by August 15, 1922.

The big offensive started on August 26, 1922, under the commands of Mustafa Kemal, General Fevzi (Çakmak), and General ‹smet (‹nönü). The Greek forces were encircled and were forced into a frenzy. Some of them were taken prisoner. Thus, the offensive achieved its end. On August 30, the Turkish forces defeated the Greeks in a pitched battle called "the Battle of the Commander in Chief" which was commanded by Mustafa Kemal. The Turkish Army continued their operation; Izmir was taken on September 9, Bursa on September 11, and finally, on September 18, the whole country was liberated from the Greek invasion.

## The Final Phase of the Conflict: The Tremendous Victory of Mustafa Kemal

The final thing to do for Mustafa Kemal was to liberate Istanbul, the Straits of Dardanelles and Bosporus, and eastern Thrace. However, the tension between the Turkish and British troops was aroused when Lloyd George, the British Prime Minister stated that this would be a reason for a *casus belli*. This time the war might break out between Britain and Turkey, as British occupation troops were pinned down at Chanak (Çanakkale), a small seaport on the Dardanelles. On September 15, Britain sent a telegram calling upon the Dominions to contribute soldiers in a demonstration of the Empire's solidarity against the Turks. This crisis was called the "Chanak Affair". The next day the request was made public, resulting in a breach of imperial etiquette and political good sense. As a matter of fact, the French and Italians left Britain alone in this matter. The British public also did not want to go to war, as the Turks guaranteed not to close the Straits to them. Then the crises quickly ended.

### Peace Talks

After the victories of the Turkish army, Allied powers began to discuss a truce with Mustafa Kemal. Then the Mudanya Armistice signed on October 11, 1922, which led the way to Lausanne. According to the Mudanya Armistice, the Greeks would evacuate eastern Thrace within 15 days and this area would be returned to the Turks. The Allied forces at the Bosporus and Istanbul would stay until the peace treaty was signed. Turkey, which had been under foreign occupation since the Mudros Armistice, was rescued from invasion. It was time for a meeting to discuss the terms of the Peace Treaty. As a matter of fact, the Allied powers had the Ottoman government sign the Sevres Peace Treaty as a finalizing act of the First World War. The *GNA* not only had opposed it however, but had also gone through a series of battles in order to not apply its terms. The nationalists with their leader Mustafa Kemal made the Treaty of Sevres unworkable. The Lausanne negotiations began in Switzerland on November 20, 1922 for a replacement Treaty.

Lausanne resulted in the opening of negotiations on a more equal footing.

At this point, the Allies invited both the Ottoman government in Istanbul and the National government in Ankara to Lausanne in order to play one against the other. There seemed to be two governments in Turkey, one in Ankara, the other in Istanbul. The dual appearances could also have put the country's integrity in danger. Mustafa Kemal took this opportunity to abolish the sultanate, as it had already been outmoded. The sultanate was abolished on November 1, 1922, this marked the official end of the Ottoman Empire. Yet as the Ottoman sultans were also Caliphs, Abdulmecid was appointed Caliph as Mehmed VI was removed from the position of sultan. The Ottoman dynasty kept the Caliphate power in its own hands. The *GNA* however, became the single authority in the country.

Peace negotiations between Turkey and the Allied powers began at a conference held in Lausanne on November 20, 1922. The Turkish delegation was led by ‹smet Bey (‹nönü). Though the conference broke down on February 4, 1923, it re-started on the 23rd April. While Turkish delegates insisted on the terms of the National Oath of 1920, the Allied powers were much keener on the terms of the Sevres Treaty. The main quarrels were over the questions of the Ottoman debts, capitulations, the Status of the Turkish Straits and the Iraqi frontier.

Following long discussions, an agreement was reached in Lausanne on July 24, 1923. The treaty provided for the independence of the Republic of Turkey, and it marked the international recognition of Mustafa Kemal's government in Ankara and the new Turkish state. It was a tremendous victory for the Turks who gained complete independence. The capitulations were abolished. There would not be any Armenian or Kurdish autonomous state, nor any form of political formation in eastern Turkey. Western Anatolia would also not be a part of Greek territory. Mustafa Kemal almost achieved the objectives of the National Oath of 1920. However, some problems like Mosul, Hatay (Alexandretta Province), and the Straits could not be solved at the conference as it was envisaged in the National Oath. Great Britain insisted that Mosul should be returned to Iraq, although the Mudros Armistice suggested the opposite. The Turkish Straits were demilitarized and its administrations would be carried out by an international commission. Turkey did not insist on these points in order to reach a peaceful conclusion, which it desperately needed. They thought that these problems might be overcome through diplomatic channels after a considerable amount of time.

# CHAPTER 12

## The Founding of the Turkish Republic

After Turkey's military and political achievements, two more important (but expected decisions) were made: the first was the proclaiming of Ankara as Turkey's capital on October 13, 1923. The second was the *GNA*'s declaration of the Republic on October 29, 1923. Then the *GNA* selected Mustafa Kemal, who had had a great role in founding the new state, as the first President of the Turkish Republic. Mustafa Kemal is the founder of Modern Turkey. Turkish people gave him the surname "Atatürk", meaning the ancestor of the Turks.

### A. The Atatürk Era (1923 - 1938):
### Atatürk's Basic Reforms

Atatürk charged İsmet İnönü with the establishment of the cabinet. Then Atatürk carried out a serious of revolutionary reforms in order to create a modern state based on democratic and secular principles. The *GNA* accepted a law on March 3, 1924 which abolished the Caliphate. On the same day, the law concerning the abolition of the Ministry for Religious Affairs and the Foundations (*Waqfs*), and the law concerning the unification of education were promulgated. In order to organize the religious affairs of the society, the Presidency of Religious Affairs was established. To meet the requirements of religious personnel, a faculty of Theology was open at the *Darulfunun*, renamed Istanbul University in 1933. Thus, all the schools controlled by the Ministry for Religious Affairs and the Ministry of Foundations were closed. With the unification of instructions, all schools were brought under the control of the Ministry of National Education in accordance with national and secular principles. One of Atatürk's main goals was to modernize the Turkish state and society. To do so, he had to struggle to promote the modern educational system. Therefore, a number of schools and faculties were founded in the 1930s.

On April 20, 1924, the new Constitution that reorganized the state was promulgated by the Turkish Grand National Assembly. The reforms of the Trade Penal Law started during the Tanzimat period and continued as the principles of Sharia

(Islamic Law), were abolished. On April 4, 1926, Turkish Civil Code, then the others, came into force. With the Turkish Civil Code, Turkish women gained basic rights and reached a new milestone on the road of progress. The Municipal Act of 1930 and the National Assembly Act of 1934 granted suffrage to Turkish women. Thus, the Turkish woman possessed almost all basic political rights.

In 1928, the phrase "Islam is the official religion of the state" was removed from the Constitution in accordance with secular principles. The Turkish Constitution of 1937 established the basic principle of bringing Turkey into line with the standards of modern civilization and secularism.

## Abortive Attempt at a Multi-Party System

Due to the fact that Atatürk's aim was to promote a political system based on democracy, he established the People's Party on September 9, 1923, then renamed it as the Republican People's Party (*RPP*) following the declaration of the Republic. Of course, political parties are one of the main principles of a democratic system. Turkey had some experience with political parties since 1908, as some parties were founded during the Second Constitutional period. However, the Party of Union and Progress took power by force in 1913 and then established its own dictatorship, which created the single-party system.

After the founding of the Republic, the new state had to face a number of internal and external problems. Discussion of the problems led some MPs to depart from the *RPP*. Some of those who resigned from the *RPP*, like Kazım Karabekir, Refet Bele and Rauf Orbay, were Atatürk's colleagues during the National Struggle. They established a new party called the Progressive Republican Party (*PRP*) which was the first opposition party of the Republic headed by Kazım Karabekir. On domestic policy, the party was generally regarded as being Islamic-oriented. In fact, the party's slogan was respectful towards religious principles, and gathered those who opposed Atatürk's basic modernization principles. The Progressive Republican Party's program threatened the unity of Turkey, as this opposition provoked a number of unwanted events. During this time - while Turkey was occupied with the Mosul question (which could not be concluded at the Lausanne negotiations) - a rebellion led by Sheikh Said erupted in the east. Sheikh Said's rebellion was suppressed with great difficulty on May 31, 1925. It was decided that the *PRP*'s policy had encouraged the rebellion and separatist activities in Turkey. The party was closed on June 5, 1925. The first attempt in Atatürk's time to create a multi-party system failed.

Atatürk was quite aware of the fact that the single-party system was not compatible with the democratic system. Although the first attempt failed, he asked his close associate Fethi Okyar to establish a new party to appease the discontent spawned by economic problems and the government's radical programs. Fethi Okyar returned from his post of ambassador to France to assume the leadership of the party. He established the Free Republican Party on August 12, 1930. Okyar's party promoted a liberal economic policy and was respectful of the secular and democratic principles of Kemalist thought. Yet when religious elements and others began to organize around the Free Republican Party, Fethi Okyar realized the threat that this posed to the regime and therefore ended his party on November 17, 1930. Though a multi-party system could not be established in his time, Atatürk preferred keeping a democracy; at least he did not give up the parliament system. One should not forget the fact that dictators were prevailing all over the world in the same period.

### Atatürk's Foreign Policy

The diplomatic relations with imperialist powers, which were established by Atatürk following the successful conclusion of the National Struggle against them, should be given a great deal of importance. The world in Atatürk's time, indeed, was being dragged towards crisis as liberalism was on the verge of bankruptcy and dictatorial and tyrannical regimes were prevailing over most of Europe. Taking this into consideration, the emergence of a leader such as Atatürk was a chance not only for Turkey, but for the whole world. Atatürk, who had struggled against western imperialist powers to defend his country for a considerable time, chose to found a western-style political system. Thus he became one of the few world leaders who advocated peace and insisted on using diplomacy to solve problems.

The objectives of the Nationalist Movement had been largely reached by the Lausanne Treaty of 1923, which marked the legal acceptance of modern Turkey's existence, as recognized by the entire international community. Yet for the first time in her history, Turkey was deprived of her full sovereignty over the Straits, the security of which had so concerned the Great Powers. Atatürk's Turkey was far from satisfied so long as the Straits commission and the de-militarized zones existed, since the Straits issue was closely related to the objective of being a fully sovereign country. At the same time, Turkey could not have insisted on a more final resolution at Lausanne, with British warships menacingly anchored outside Istanbul. For the moment, Turkey had to bide her time. Tevfik Rüştü Aras, one of the Turkish delegates of the National Assembly involved in the Lausanne negotiations and later Foreign Minister, pointed out that after long discussion it was concluded that though the Straits Convention did not conflict with the National Pact of 1920, the clauses referring to the de-militarization of the Straits would obviously leave Turkey in an insecure position. To reach a peaceful settlement however, so long as the four powers (Great Britain, France, Italy and Japan) guaranteed the Straits' security and the possibility of a military establishment just outside the zones, this would provide necessary military measures.

Indeed, the line taken by Turkish foreign policy makers, mainly Atatürk, was the consequence of their experiences from Ottoman days and the post-1918 struggle of the Turkish National Movement, which to some extent led to the adoption of a foreign policy based on pragmatism and non-adventurism. After the dismemberment of the Ottoman Empire, the Kemalist elite had been determined to establish a nation state based on contemporary Western models. The context of a pragmatic approach to foreign policy also dictated that a peaceful environment was needed to carry out reforms at home. This was part of a modernization process aimed at complete political, economic and ideological independence in order to align Turkey with the West, as well as remedy her economic weakness. In

fact, the leading decision-making elite was quite aware of the fact that their stance was the only way to achieve a peaceful atmosphere in such a region, geographically located as it was at the crossroads between East and West where the Great Powers had huge interests, particularly Great Britain and the Soviet Union (*USSR*).

A few months after the Lausanne settlement, Turkey's main concern in foreign affairs was to solve the outstanding problems left by the Lausanne settlement. One of them, the bitter Mosul dispute with Britain, was concluded in the latter's favor by the Council of the League of Nations on December 16, 1925. The Council's decision inevitably led to a revitalizing of the relationship between Turkey and the *USSR*. In fact, the two countries signed a treaty of friendship the day after the Council's decisions on the Mosul dispute. This agreement was not based upon ideological affinity, since Westernization was one of the main principles of modern Turkey and was incompatible with Bolshevism. Nevertheless, the circumstances of the time made Turkey more vulnerable to Soviet economic and political support since the Soviet Union tried to take advantage of them in order to impose her political influence on Turkey. Indeed, this was justified by Turkey's slow rapprochement with the West, which began after the solution of the Mosul dispute with the signing of the Anglo-Turkish Treaty on June 6, 1926.

Given that territorial integrity and complete freedom were paramount to Kemalist Turkey from its inception, the country looked on the Lausanne Straits Convention as an unsatisfactory settlement which infringed her independence, exposed her to serious attack, and diminished her value in the world of international diplomacy. Turkey did not feel secure as a consequence of the Convention, therefore she sought a way to minimize its effects. A new road was constructed within the zones in order to allow Turkey to mobilize her army in the demilitarized zone and install artillery just outside or even within the zones, as well as laying mines at the outlet of the Dardanelles and entrance to the Bosporus in order to be able to close the Straits in the event of any aggression. Even so, for Turkey it was a far from satisfactory solution since the Lausanne Settlement left Turkey in a position dependent friendship with the Soviet Union.

The close relationship with the *USSR*, although lasting less than a decade, showed that Soviet policy regarding the Straits was no different from Tsarist policy. The Soviets still continued to pressurize Turkey to secure a better position in defiance of the Lausanne Settlement. For instance, contrary to the Lausanne Convention, the *USSR* proposed to the Turkish government that, in a war where the *USSR* was a belligerent, the Straits should be closed to all belligerent warships as a kind of joint defense measure. In other words, Moscow tried by one means or another to take advantage of having a good relationship with Turkey. In line with this, the Soviet government sought to set up Turkey as a barrier between herself and the rest of the naval powers, particularly Britain.

However, the approach of the *USSR* was not welcomed by Turkish policy makers because it was thought that having a good relationship with the *USSR* put it on a higher footing, which was contrary to the principles of Kemalist foreign policy. Therefore, the Kemalist elite were determined to establish relationships with the Western countries based on equality, through which Turkey could gain a more secure place in the region. They were also aware of the fact that every major conflict with the Western countries would give the *USSR* a dominant position towards Turkey, following the experience of the Mosul dispute. Clearly, Turkey would not enjoy the *USSR* becoming a dominating presence along her frontier. Instead, Turkish foreign policy makers followed the policy of establishing a good relationship with the West and all neighbors in order to take a respected place in world diplomacy as a regional power. In addition, it was believed that having a good relationship with the West would lessen Soviet pressure on Turkey. In this regard, friendship with Great Britain would be the best pragmatic foreign policy approach.

As a first step, Turkey established good relationships with all her neighbors by signing friendship agreements which solved frontier questions, and tried to orient her foreign policy to the West. With this in mind, Turkey reached agreement with Britain over Mosul rather than fight for the disputed territory. After long insistence on the preservation of a regime of capitulations, and compensation for the debts which resulted from Turkey's previous economic penetration by the West, France finally came to an agreement with Turkey regulating financial and economic matters in June 1928. Pursuing the line of improving relations with the West, Turkey signed a neutrality agreement with Italy in May 1928 and the difficult relationship with Greece was also normalized in June 1930. Parallel agreements were concluded with the eastern countries of Iraq, Iran and Afghanistan and the Balkan countries of Albania, Bulgaria and Yugoslavia during the same period.

All the same, the period between Lausanne and early 1930 was primarily one of introspection, foreign policy was of secondary importance. Turkey was fully occupied in defining her national identity and making domestic reforms, it had little time for outside distractions. By early 1930 however, Turkey was beginning to follow a more active foreign policy. Turkey turned its attention towards international organizations and began attending bilateral and multinational meetings in which priority was given to the Straits settlement. Turkey in fact took every opportunity to point out how the demilitarized Straits zones not only put Turkey's security in a dangerous position but also threatened regional peace. There is little doubt that this resulted from a growing recognition of Turkey's main external threat: fascist Italy's ambition to militarily dominate the eastern Mediterranean and Anatolia. Indeed, immediately after the First World War it became clear that the Versailles peace system only exacerbated the complex of nationalistic sentiments which had bedeviled all of Europe. The struggle to create an international security system to uphold the status quo established by the peace treaties was frustrated by the countries that were dissatisfied with the post-war settlement.

Mustafa Kemal Atatürk believed that another major conflict was imminent. He remarked in his conversation with General McArthur in 1931 that the Treaty of Versailles had not removed any of the causes which had led to the First World War. On the contrary, it had only deepened the rift between the former rivals. In the case of a renewed conflict, as far as Turkish security was concerned, the Turkish Straits would be in the most vulnerable position. Therefore now was the time to take more decisive steps before it was too late in order to put Turkey in a more secure position. Unlike the method chosen by ex-enemy states, the Turkish government was determined to attain its goal through diplomacy. In this sense, the acceptance of Turkey into the League of Nations in 1932 can be regarded as a huge Turkish success to escape not only from diplomatic isolation (into which Turkey had been forced by the Western countries after the First World War) but also from dependency upon the *USSR*. Yet as Anglo-Turkish relations gradually improved, Soviet-Turkish relationships gradually deteriorated. Fearing, no doubt, an increase in British influence over the Straits, the Soviet government reverted to the policy of imperial Russia and sought an alliance with Turkey which gave the *USSR* a military base on the Straits. Growing Soviet pressure together with the deteriorating situation in the eastern Mediterranean caused by Italy accelerated the Turkish rapprochement to the Western powers to whom she appealed for a revision of the current Straits regime.

## The Hope of Peace

Turkey attached substantial importance to securing Great Britain's support in the revision, since it would make a positive outcome all the more likely. In this respect, it was widely accepted that the year 1934 would mark the beginning of a new phase of rapprochement in Anglo-Turkish relations with the appointment of Sir Percy Loraine as British Ambassador to Ankara and Fethi Okyar, Atatürk's close friend, to London as Turkish Ambassador. Loraine gained the personal friendship of Atatürk, partly by playing poker all night. Obviously Atatürk desired to see some concrete sign of friendship, which he had been after for years. Though Loraine appealed to the Foreign Office to strengthen ties with Turkey, London was reluctant to take any further steps at this stage considering that this would mean some kind of security engagement which Britain, only just rearming, could not afford. Nevertheless this process led to an atmosphere of greater understanding between the two countries.

In the face of Italy's aggressive intentions which had also targeted Turkey, Ankara increased her feverish action to enhance its security through diplomatic channels. The formation of a defensive Balkan Pact between the four Balkan countries of Yugoslavia, Romania, Greece and Turkey on February 9, 1934 added impetus to the growing pressure for a comprehensive revision of the post-war settlement. One of Turkey's aims in forming the Balkan pact was to invite Bulgaria into the pact so that Bulgaria would be separated from Italy. Despite the refusal of the Bulgarians to come into the pact, Turkey largely secured the support of the rest of the Balkan countries concerning the Straits issue.

By the middle of March 1936 the Straits question entered a new phase due to further challenges to the Versailles system which had provided Turkey with favorable grounds for her claim, namely the increasingly successful Italian campaign in Abyssinia in violation of the League Covenant, and the German reoccupation of the de-militarized zone of the Rhineland on March 7, 1936 in violation of the Treaties of Versailles and Locarno, which seriously damaged the prestige of international law. In these circumstances, Turkey appeared to be a good example of a country who would be able to show that treaty revision by agreement rather than by force was still be possible, and in Rendel's (head of the Eastern Department in the British Foreign Office) words it would "offer us almost our only real hope of peace." Then Turkey was encouraged to raise the question of remilitarization of the Straits once again. Subsequent developments allowed Turkey to become the guardian of the Straits by the Montreux Convention of 1936. This was a tremendous diplomatic achievement for Turkey. This was the result of Atatürk's insistence on staying with diplomacy.

During 1937, indications of Atatürk's worsening health began to appear. While he was on a trip to Yalova during the first months of 1938 he encountered a serious illness. Atatürk, founder of modern Turkey, died on November 10, 1938 at the age of 57.

## B. The İnönü Era (1938 - 1950)

The day after Atatürk's death, İsmet İnönü was elected as the second president. He also assumed the leadership of the Republican People's Party. İnönü remained the president of the Turkish Republic until May 1950. At the general nationwide congress of the *RPP* on December 26, 1938, İsmet İnönü was elected as the "everlasting *RPP* leader" after the Atatürk era. The delegates gave Atatürk the title of Eternal Chief, and to İnönü the title of National Chief. According to the single-party system, there was a cordial relationship between the party and the state apparatus because the President was the Republican People's party chairman at the same time. The minister of Home Affairs was the General Secretary of the Party at the same time, and the governors were the Party's local leaders in the provinces. So İnönü firmly controlled both of party and the state apparatus, and did not give any opportunity to raise a second man. Therefore, Turkey's foreign and domestic policies were under his control. At the extraordinary Party Congress of May 29, 1939, in the absence of any opposition party, the Independent Group (*Müstakil Group*) was established within the MPs of the *RPP* in order to freely criticize government policy. However, the group could not act as opposition members; rather instead they acted as members of the RPP since any member of the Group did not raise any serious objections against government policy, though some other members of the *RPP* did.

It can be said that the reason for İnönü's policy of taking all power in his hands was not totally his desire to create his own dictatorship, but rather his eagerness to maintain Atatürk's reforms. One should not forget the fact that when İnönü came to power the Second World War was about to start. Another thing is that, in the absence of democratic experience, coming to power after a charismatic leader such as Atatürk, it was not easy to take political power under his own control for he did not have a charismatic character as the ex-leader did. The gains of the Republic could have been lost in the face of growing dissident. In the end, it was İnönü who voluntarily gave up all his titles after the war and who introduced the multi-party system.

Turkey's foreign and domestic policy during the time of İnönü was mostly shaped under the conditions of the Second World War. Though Turkey did not enter the war, its army was in a state of alert. Much of the Turkish national budget was allotted to military expenditure. In order to overcome the economic strain, the government issued a law on January 18, 1940 called the National Protection Law (*Milli Korunma Kanunu*). This law prevented any possible economic turmoil caused by the war. However, this was a failure. The second attempt to restore the economic situation was to prevent wealthy citizens who were, according to the government, trying to make a profit from the war conditions by using the black market and stockpiling. The government thought that they were not taxed in accordance with their income. The government, who was looking for a new source of revenues, diverted its attention to those who were wealthy, many of whom were non-Muslim, and issued a law on November 11, 1942 called the Wealth Tax, or, Capital Tax (*Varlık Vergisi*). This law served to raise funds for the country's defense in the eventuality of war. It was imposed on fixed assets, such as landed estates, building owners, real estate brokers, and businesses and industrial enterprises of all citizens, including minorities. Those who could not pay their taxes were sent to labor camps. The government decisions were criticized however, because those who suffered most severely were non-Muslims. Finally, the government abandoned the applications of the Wealth Tax on March 15, 1944.

Not only wealthy people suffered from the government policy. Turkish peasants were also forced to pay levies with a law issued on May 15, 1943 for Agriculture Products. The situation in the rural areas was much worse than in the urban ones. Therefore, some claim that the Agriculture Products Law was to complete the Wealth Tax.

### Cultural Projects

One of İnönü's projects was the founding of the Village Institute in 1940. This was the cornerstone of the rural development project. Its aim was to train rural people to become teachers in villages. There was a lack of schools in rural areas at this time. It was thought that this lack was due to urban teachers' inability to accommodate to life in rural areas. In most of the newly formed Village Institutes students built all the school buildings themselves and farmed their own food. Their education included both practical subjects such as agriculture, construction, arts and crafts; and classical subjects such as mathematics, science, literature and history. These schools fitted with the one-party system, but they could not live in the multi-party system and were closed in 1954.

Another cultural project was the People's Houses and the People's Rooms. These were first opened in the cities and then in the villages. Their purpose was to educate the elderly through conferences, seminars and other activities. The first People's Houses had been opened by Atatürk in 1932 in the cities. İnönü extended them to the rural areas under the name of People's Rooms in 1940. The People's Rooms were relatively smaller than the People's Houses. In order to promote cultural life and to make people familiar with the Republic's ideology, the People's House in Ankara issued a quarterly magazine called *Ülkü* (a name given by Atatürk) from February 1933 to August 1950. Then the other People's Houses issued magazines in the same style as *Ülkü*, but with different names. Considering that a great percentage of Turkish people were illiterate at the time, the magazines might not have been well-suited for educating people. Therefore an organization called the People's Orators was founded within the structure of the People's Houses.

The People's Houses and the People's Rooms became a part of the Republican People's Party's establishment in İnönü's time. Their activities were suited for the one-party system. These establishments were closed when the Democratic Party came to power in 1950 under the pretext that they had departed from their original objectives.

## The Second World War and Turkish Foreign Policy

Atatürk had realized that the second major world conflict would be of immense proportions. He had wanted to form an alliance with Britain, France and the Soviet Union in order to deter Hitler's and Mussolini's expansionist policies in Central Europe and the eastern Mediterranean. Yet Britain had refuted Atatürk's offer of an alliance as it was pursuing a policy of appeasement towards Italy and Germany. It took considerable time for Britain to understand that its policy of conciliation and appeasement towards Italy and Germany only encouraged their plans to politically and economically dominate southeastern Europe and the eastern Mediterranean. Germany occupied Czechoslovakia on March 15, 1939 and subsequently threatened Poland and Romania Britain then abandoned its policy of conciliation with the fascist states, and sought an alliance almost in the line with what Atatürk had suggested. When the tension was at its peak and both blocks, namely the Democratic West and the Fascists, were looking for alliances Atatürk was replaced by İnönü as the former died a few months before the war erupted.

İnönü continued searching for an alliance with the Western countries. However Turkey insisted that the *USSR* must count in the alliance since it would be ineffective without the *USSR*. It can be said that anxiety over the Soviet Union was one of the main considerations behind Turkish foreign policy in World War II. Considering the *USSR*'s long held aspiration of gaining access to the Turkish Straits, Turkey was careful not to give the Soviets any excuse for mounting an assault. In the mean time, Germany had its own plan for Turkey, whose economy significantly depended on Germany. Franz von Papen, the new German Ambassador to Ankara, tried to prevent further Turkish moves towards western alliances by reverting to the question of Turkish neutrality. If Turkey did not remain neutral, he threatened that Germany would stop all economic and cultural co-operation.

Germany's step in escaping from western encirclement did not remain limited to detaching Turkey from a possible western alliance. Germany had begun her quest for a pact with the USSR in the spring of 1939, in order to prevent an Anglo-Soviet and French alliance and Soviet intervention in the event of a Polish-German War. Indeed, German-Soviet negotiations went on behind closed doors until they announced their conclusion in a non-aggression pact on August 23, 1939. Turkey was in a dilemma since it could no longer be both pro-Ally and pro-Soviet. Nor could it take sides without grave risks. Turkey's main plan was established on the assumption that the *USSR* would take part in the western alliance. However, Ankara did not lose her hope yet. On one hand, it maintained its negotiations with France and Britain for a pact, on the other hand it attempted a final move to bring the *USSR* to the Western side as Sükrü Saraçoglu, Turkish Minister for Foreign Affairs, visited Moscow on September 26, 1939 in order to find out Moscow's intention.

Surprisingly the Soviet government simultaneously invited the German Foreign Minister to Moscow. Thus the Soviet government wanted to improve their bargaining power against both countries.

Nothing came from Saraçoglu's Moscow visit. From then on, the Turkish government believed that the Soviet government was determined to follow Russia's age-old ambitions of obtaining the Straits by one means or another. Thus Turkey established a policy of not engaging in any commitment with the Soviet Union that might endanger Turkey's position internationally. This policy was made evident in the Tripartite Pact, signed on October 19, 1939, in which protocol II exempted Turkey from action involving her in hostilities with the *USSR*.

The issue of Turkey's participation in the war on the side of the Allies was a subject of great interest to Britain, particularly to Churchill. Turkish policy in the Second World War, however, was to play for time and pray that she would not be involved in the war, at least, she hoped, not until her rearmament had reached a stage where she would have a greater chance of resisting a German attack. Moreover, Turkey's hope and struggle for making a quadruple alliance among France, Britain and the *USSR* against Hitler failed as the *USSR* took the German side. French withdrawal from the war after defeating Germany at the very beginning of the war on the one hand, and Soviet and German pressure on the other made the Turkish government convinced to stay out of the war.

Turkey was not a military power at the time of the war, but it occupied an important geo-strategic and geo-political place for the belligerent powers' war strategies. When the German army expanded up to Bulgaria's border with Turkey in March 1941, and occupied the Aegean Islands in May, no need to mention the Italian presence in the Dodecanese Islands since 1912, Turkey's stance in the war became paramount for both sides. Then Hitler preferred occupying Russia on June 22, 1941 rather than reaching the Middle East through Turkey. This did not mean that the threat was over for Turkey, as its western boundaries were surrendered by German troops.

Both of the belligerent powers pressured Turkey to provide necessary facilities for their warships, to stop enemy passage through the Straits, and to open up their air bases and ports for their own usage. The nature of Turkey's strategic location made Ankara's friendship mandatory. Turkey remained a neutral country until the very last moment of the war, yet it carried an importance well beyond its means as a small power with a limited military potential as it resisted the pressures of all the larger powers. Turkey had no intention to embark on an adventurist policy as it had done in the First World War. Besides, held no new territorial ambitions to fulfill through war. Turkey needed more time to carry out the Kemalist reforms in order to integrate Turkey into the modern world.

As a matter of fact, the Germans had promised Turkey to make some amendments in its favor on its frontier in return for their co-operation. The Turkish government however, had no claims on their neighbors at that time. German propaganda that sought to unite the Turkish populations within the *USSR* did not respond well with official circles, though some within the Pan-Turkist movements were keen on that idea. The Turkish policy makers in that time were aware that there was no room for such ideological claims in real politics. Particularly İnönü, who was the main figure of Turkish foreign policy, did not give any credit to those who were after an adventurous policy in the line stated above.

Turkish foreign policy in this war may not be accurately defined as strictly neutral. The best definition of the Turkish stance is *non-belligerency,* or *benevolent neutrality* as Selim Deringil points out. First of all Turkey, from at the very beginning, took the side of the Allies by signing the Tri-partite Pact. In the war Turkey gave some considerable support to the Allies beyond neutrality. One might claim that Turkey held a pro-German stance as it signed a Friendship Agreement with Germany on June 18, 1941 which facilitated the German invasion of the USSR (code name *Operation Barbarossa*) on June 22. However, Turkey had no other choice but to sign it. Otherwise a German invasion would have been unavoidable: an invasion which Turkey had no modernized army to counter. It was not what Britain wanted though.

Turkey wholeheartedly wanted the Western Block to win the war. But, Soviet co-operation with Britain, following *Operation Barborassa*, raised the question of post-war role of the Soviet Union in Turkish official circles. This does not mean that Turkey's choice was the Nazis. For Turkish authorities, the Nazis' aim was not that different from the *USSR*'s. Great Britain could not supply the Turkish army in order to be able to fight against the well-equipped German army. The best thing for the Turkish government to do was to stay out of the war as much as possible. It was what İnönü was doing. Although Turkey's stance was pro-Allies, it had to make some concessions to the Germans.

Turkey's position was understandable for Britain until 1943, as Turkey's neutral stance benefited them as well. Yet as the situation shifted in favor of the Allies they put pressure on Turkey to enter into the war on their side. To do so, Churchill came to Adana, a Turkish province in the Eastern Mediterranean region, on January 30 - February 1, 1943 to discuss Turkish entry into the war with İnönü and Saraçoglu, now Prime Minister. Churchill wanted Turkey to enter the war at the end of the year in return for supplying the armaments which Turkey required. At this point the Allies' opinion about Turkey's participation in the war was a matter of discussion. Some of them wanted Turkey's co-operation in the form of giving the Allies authorization to use bases in Turkey, rather than an active military participation. Others, particularly the USSR, wanted active military involvement. Following long diplomatic meetings, İnönü agreed to Turkey's joining the war "in principle" at the Cairo meeting on December 4 - 8, 1943. The President demanded excessive war equipment to modernize his army, but this demand was accepted by the Allies. At this time Moscow was reluctant for Turkey's involvement in the war, in their opinion, it was too late. This attitude only sharpened Turkey's suspicion about post-war Soviet intentions in Turkey. Finally, Turkey did not join the war because the time was over.

The political line taken by Turkey was protested by Britain and the USA, and relationships with Turkey broke down in early 1944. The latest developments were obviously not in Turkey's favor as the Allies were preparing for Operation Overlord, the code name given by the Allies for the Normandy invasion. Turkey finally began to agree to the Allies' terms in June 1944. On August 2nd, Turkey broke its diplomatic and economic relationships with Germany, as the Allies had wanted. To do so, Turkey was guaranteed that it would be treated as an allied country at the end of the war. The USSR obviously was not happy with that. When the Allies met at the Yalta Conference in February 4 - 11, 1945, Stalin raised the modification of the Montreux Convention of 1936 which was regulating the passage of foreign warships in and out of the Black Sea, but neither the American nor the British delegations were in favor of the Soviet demands. Another important decision that pertained to Turkey at the Yalta Conference was the invitation to the San Francisco Conference to those who had broken diplomatic relationships with Germany, without actually having taken part in the war.

This proved to Turkey that Britain would not abandon it in the post-war period vis-à-vis the *USSR* for the sake of long-tem British interests in the region.

On February 23, 1945, Turkey declared war on Japan and Germany as decided at Yalta in order to be able to attend the San Francisco Conference that established the United Nations (UN). Therefore, Turkey was one of the founding members of the UN. In the end Turkey seemingly succeeded in taking part on the winning side even though it stayed out of the war.

## Turkey's Transition Period to Liberal Democracy (1945-50)

Though Turkey did not enter the Second World War it was adversely affected by it. Throughout the war a large army was kept alert and ready, prices increased rapidly, many of the basic food items were rationed, and many items could not be found or were sold on the black market. A large social reaction stemming from the problems of the war was aroused against the *RPP*, whose social and economic projects did not meet the people's demands, particularly in the rural areas. Furthermore, a strong opposition movement appeared from within the *RPP* that complained about the oppressive management of the party and wanted more freedom and democracy. The tolerant attitude of President İnöı ü also encouraged this movement, as he could not remain aloof from the social dissidents. In fact, he first mentioned the necessity of "liberalizing the regime" in 1945. Subsequently, he started talking about "the need for an opposition party".

There were also external factors behind İnönü's democratization move. Turkey was afraid of being isolated from the free world due to its neutrality in the Second World War. Isolation meant leaving Turkey alone to face the Soviets, who put great pressure on Turkey with demands for military bases and joint defense in the Turkish Straits. Turkey could not do anything against these Soviet demands without backing from the outside. To obtain Western support Turkey hastened to transition to the multi-party system, as the single-party system was not compatible with post-war western democratic practices.

There is little doubt that the movement that started the transition period stemmed from the opposition inside the *RPP*. Four members of the *RPP*, Celal Bayar, Atatürk's last Prime Minister, Refik Koraltan, Fuat Köprülü, and Adnan Menderes filed a famous motion to the Parliamentary Group of the RPP, which was later referred to as the Quartet Motion. They wanted to change the party regulations and some of the laws. Following the refusal of their motion, Bayar resigned from the RPP and from the Parliament. Menderes, Köprülü, and Koraltan were expelled from the party for not conforming to party discipline.

Bayar, Menderes, Köprülü, and Koraltan established the Democratic Party (*DP*) on January 7, 1946. The establishment of a new party was met with enthusiasm by the people who had become tired of the oppressive policies of single party rule. The *DP* defended a liberal economic approach and democracy. It developed rapidly in a short period of time. The first Turkish opposition party however, was the National Development Party (*NDP*) which was established on July 18, 1945. It did not flourish as did the *DP*. In 1946, eleven other parties were established in addition to the *DP* and the *NDP*.

The establishment of so many parties pushed the RPP to re-evaluate its democratic program. On May 10, 1946, İnönü gave up the titles of Eternal Chief and National Chief in an extraordinary Party Congress. The Independent Group within the RPP was abolished, the election system was revised, and laws concerning the press were liberalized.

In the meantime, the *DP* succeeded in entering Parliament in the 1946 elections. In the elections of May 14, 1950 the *DP* came to power. Thus, the single party period ended in Turkey and for the first time a change in power was realized with the votes of the people. Celal Bayar was selected as President of Turkey by the Parliament. Then Bayar charged Adnan Menderes with forming a cabinet.

Thus the twenty-seven year old *RPP* government was replaced by the DP via democratic methods. This was a milestone in Turkish democracy. Thereafter, Turkey experienced and still experiences a multi-party political system. However, Turkish democracy ran into difficulties great enough to impel democracy to intervene 'to save democracy'. Military intervention happened twice in the 1960s and 1980s. The government was taken over and a new democratic system was instituted. Turkish democracy was affected by a coup via a memorandum in 1971, forcing a change of government. In 1997, the Turkish military exerted pressure through the National Security Council to save the secular state from allegedly being undermined by the Religious Welfare Party that dominated the government. Although these military interventions interrupted democracy, it did not create any alternative system to democracy.

## C. Turkish Foreign Policy in the Cold War (1945 - 1990)

As Hitler's defeat removed the chief raison d'être of the Grand Alliance between the Western countries and the *USSR*, each country followed its own policy towards the end of the war. The *USA* and the *USSR* emerged as superpowers whose world-wide interests divided the world into two blocks. These two strategic and ideological blocks were the democratic west led by the *USA*, and the communist east led by the *USSR*. This led to the onset of the Cold War. During this period, countries were forced to join one of the camps in accordance with their affinity.

Turkey's decision to join the Western Camp in the post war period was inevitable since neutrality was not seen as a viable option for Turkey who was under Soviet pressure with demands of military bases in the Straits. İnönü was eager to adopt foreign policy based on close co-operation with the United States. In the initial phase, Turkey's strategic importance in the Middle Eastern area was not well assessed by the *USA*. Turkey's admission to the alliance was slow in coming, but nonetheless was complete when it did come. The visit to Istanbul of the US warship Missouri in 1946, the start of the first military and economic aid from America with the implementation of the Truman Doctrine in 1947 and the Marshall Plan in 1948 strengthened the Western-oriented foundations of Turkish foreign policy, which had been laid by İnönü and then maintained by the DP. Turkey's western orientation continued in its active involvement in the 1950-1953 Korean War, and by becoming a *NATO* member on February 17, 1952. Turkey kept its unique position in the Western Security System during the Cold War period. The Straits were of particular importance in the Cold War for neutralizing the Soviet submarine threat in the Mediterranean. Therefore, Turkey provided the security of the southeastern flank of *NATO*.

Economic and security considerations were the main factors in Turkey's relationship with the West in the Cold War period. Yet Turkey's affinity to the West, as far as its foreign policy is concerned, might be seen as the continuance of the westernization and modernization process. Sometimes Turkey's foreign policy makers went too far in unilaterally allying themselves with the West (particularly during the *DP*'s time in office). This unilateral support for the West weakened Turkey vis-à-vis the West. For example, the *DP* became actively involved in Middle Eastern in order accordance with the interests of western foreign policy, and it showed great enthusiasm to co-operate with the *USA* in Middle Eastern affairs.

Though the *DP* government signed an agreement with the *USA* in which Turkey allowed the settling of American Jupiter missiles which were targeted on the *USSR* in their territories, the Turkish government could not find American financial support. The change in East-West relations, which became more visible after the 1962 Cuban missile crisis when it became clear that both the United States and the *USSR* were determined not to be drawn into war with each other, only gradually convinced Turkish policymakers of the need for a multilateral foreign policy. From time to time, Turkey tried to pursue a multilateral foreign policy by approaching the *USSR* and the Non-Aligned nations, as it was disappointed with the attitude of its allies who failed to support Turkey in financial and foreign policy issues. Yet no Turkish governments ever tried to change its fundamentally western-orientate d foreign policy. Turkey did not or could not create an alternative foreign policy: the alternative to the *USA* in its foreign policy was the European Economic Community, later the European Union. The alternative to the West for Turkey was the West during this period.

Turkish foreign policy makers' main engagement in the Cold War period, even the post-cold war, was intensified on two issues: Cyprus and Accession in the European Community.

## The Cyprus Question

The root of the Cyprus problems for Turkey goes back to Ottoman times. In 1878, Britain temporarily took over Cyprus from the Ottoman Empire in return for its support in the Russian-Turkish War. Following the Ottoman Empire's collapse, Turkey recognized British sovereignty over Cyprus at the Lausanne Conference. Greek Cypriots however, developed a policy called "enosis" by which Cyprus would unite with Greece, as they consider Greece their motherland. As Greek Cypriots followed the enosis policy, Turkish Cypriots were organized under different organizations and parties in order to defend their rights and to prevent Cyprus from uniting with Greece. Greece also wanted to discuss the issue with Great Britain with bilateral discussions in 1954. They even guaranteed Britain a base in return for their recognizing enosis, but Britain rejected that saying that they had no Cyprus problem to discuss.

Turkey did not want to be involved in the question as long as Cyprus remained under British control. However, Turkey reserved its right to intervene if there were any changes in status quo. In the meantime, when the guerrilla movement *EOKA* was formed in Cyprus in 1955 in order to end British rule and unite the island with Greece, Britain began to discuss evacuation. *EOKA* carried out a series of terrorist acts against the Turkish Cypriots and the British. After that Turkey became a part of the question as the British implemented its plans for evacuation from the island and terrorist attacks continued against the Turkish Cypriots. After long term discussion between Greece, Britain, and Turkey, the Greek Cypriots and leadership of Greece were forced to accept the formation of an independent Cyprus in 1960. The Republic of Cyprus was set up with the Zurich Agreements of 1959 and the London Agreements of 1960. These agreements suggested a collective administration between the Turkish and Greek Cypriots: The president would be a Greek; its deputy would be a Turkish Cypriot who had the right of veto any decisions of the president. The Turks and Greek Cypriots had equal rights. Greece, Britain, and Turkey would be guarantors of the Republic. If there was any violation of the status quo that was established in 1960, any of these countries had the right to intervene alone or with the co-operation of the other two.

Archbishop Makarious, President of the Republic, did not show any willingness to put the constitution of 1960 into force. Rather, he treated the Turks as a minority, contrary to the status quo that was established in 1960. He also followed policy in line with enosis which led to a break down in the agreement of 1960. Then the Turkish Cypriots who worked in the state institutions and establishments were removed at the end of 1963. Since then Turkish Cypriots were under heavy Greek assaults on the island. When Turkey warned the Greek Cypriots that all conditions were created for Turkish intervention which was suggested in the Zurich and London agreements as the result of their cruelty towards Turkish society, ignoring the Turkish societies on the islands, U.S. president Lyndon B. Johnson warned Turkey not to do so. Then some negotiations took place between Greece and Turkey to find a diplomatic solution to the problem.

In the mean time, *EOKA-B*, a Greek Cypriot right-wing pro-enosis paramilitary organization, formed in 1971 that was supported by the ruling Greek military junta which had come to power in 1967. EOKA-B was primarily a terrorist organization that murdered civilians, and was under the direct control and influence of the military junta in Athens who had overthrown Makarios and installed Nikos Sampson in 1974 as the dictator of

Cyprus in order to achieve enosis through violent means. These developments put the Turkish Cypriots in a more insecure position which led to Turkish military intervention in 1974 provided by the Zurich and Lausanne Agreements of 1959 and 1960. Turkey intervened in order to put an end to the Greek Cypriot assaults on Turkish Cypriots. In the end the island was divided in two: Greek Cypriots in the south and Turks in the north.

Turkey was faced with an American embargo following military intervention which lasted until 1978. Since long discussions did not bring any solution, Turkish Cypriots declared their independence by establishing the Turkish Republic of Northern Cyprus on November 15, 1983. Rauf Denktaş became president of the Republic. However, no international organization or country recognizes it other than Turkey. It is interesting to note here that Turkey and Turkish Cypriots have been blamed as the ones who did not want any solution in Cyprus, though Turkey and Denktaş spent great effort to bring an end to the question. It became obvious when Turkey and the Turkish Cypriots gave great support for Kofi Annan's resolutions for the Cyprus question in a referendum simultaneously held in Northern and Southern Cyprus in April 2004 while Greek Cypriots rejected it.

### The Long Quest for European Union

Turkey first applied to join the European Economic Community in 1959 and was admitted as an Associate Member in 1963. Turkey has always wanted to be accepted as part of Europe but did not spend much effort on furthering its application for full membership mainly for economic reasons, fearing the effects of opening its market to European penetration. However, when Turgut Özal came to power in 1983 he followed a more market oriented economic policy, but his application for full membership in 1987 was rejected. Since then the relationships with the European Union have occupied a decisive and primary place in Turkish foreign policies. However, at this time some political criteria for becoming a member came into prominence at the meeting of the European Council at Copenhagen in June 1993.

In 1995 Turkey completed a Customs Union with the European Union, and celebrated this as a major step for *EU* membership, but experienced great disappointment in the European Council meeting in Luxembourg in 1997 since Turkey could not find a place among the candidate countries. After two years of frigid relations with Turkey, the European Council accepted Turkey as a candidate country in the Helsinki meeting in 1999, which normalized the relationships. Then the vigorous agenda of reform pursued by Turkey and colossal legislative efforts have been realized, which includes among others, such measures as the comprehensive Constitutional amendments of October 2001 and May 2004. Turkey's relations with the European Union took an important turn towards accession in 2004 by the opening of accession negotiations with Turkey, on October 3, 2005.

That the post-Cold War period brought remarkable changes in to the areas around Turkey forced the Turkish foreign policymakers to adjust to new global and regional circumstances. Thus Ankara promoted a multilateral foreign policy which was aimed at diplomatic rapprochement with Caucasia, Central Asia, the Balkans, and even lately with the Middle East - which have been viewed as geographic, but also as a cultural and political entity. Turkey has tried also to build good relationships with the Russian Federation with a remarkable success. This is also valid for relationships with Israel. However, this feature of Turkish foreign policy does not completely rule out co-operation with the *USA* and the *EU*, which also remain important priorities. Recently Turkey has faced with a great challenge following the Gulf Crisis in 1990, and the US-led Multi-National Force's invasion of Iraq in 2003 and subsequent events including raised instability in the Iraq. Turkey has also had to deal with the *PKK*, a terrorist organization that has carried out terrorist activities inside Turkey. Though Turkey has been seeking international support for this struggle against terrorism, great disappointment has resulted.

# Bibliography and Further Reading

- Armaoğlu, Fahir, *Siyasi Tarih (1789-1960)*, Ankara: Sevinç Matbaası, 1964.

- Bainbridge, Margaret (ed.), *Turkic People of the World*, Colombia University Press, 1993.

- Beeley, Brain W. (ed.), *Turkish Transformation: New Century New Challanges*, Huntingdon: The Eothen Press, 2002.

- Çavdar, Tevfik, *Türkiye'nin Demokrasi Tarihi (1839-1950)*, Ankara: İmge, 2004.

- Deringil, Selim, *Turkish Foreign Policy during the Second World War: an Active Neutrality*, Cambridge: Cambridge University Press, 1989.

- Ersanlı Bahar, Büşra (ed.), *Bağımsızlığın ilk Yılları: Azerbaycan, Kazakistan, Kırgızistan, Özbekistan, Türkmenistan*, Ankara: Kültür Bakanlığı, 1994.

- Findley, Carter V., *The Turks in World History*, New York: Oxford University Press, 2005.

- Finkel, Caroline, *Osman's Dream: The Story of the Ottoman Empire, 1300–1923*, John Murray, 2005.

- Halaçoğlu, Yusuf, *Ermeni Tehciri ve Göç*, İstanbul: Bab-ı Ali Kültür Yayınları, 2004.

- Hale, William, *Turkish Foreign Policy, 1774-2000*, London: Frank Cass, 2000.

- Heper, Metin, *İsmet İnönü: Yeni Bir Yorum Denemesi*, Istanbul: Tarih Vakfı Yurt Yayınları, 1999

- Hostler, Charles Warren, *The Turks of Central Asia*, London: Praeger, 1993.

- Güvenç, Bozkurt, *Türk Kimliği: Kültür Tarihinin Kaynakları*, Ankara: Kültür Bakanlığı, 1994.

- Imber, Collin, *Osmanlı Imparatorluğu 1300–1650*, İstanbul: Bilgi Üniversitesi Yayınları, 2006.

- İnalcık, Halil, *The Ottoman Empire: The Classical Age, 1300-1600*, London: Phoenix, 1994.

- İnan, S. & Haytaoğlu, E (eds.), *Yakın Dönem Türk Politik Tarihi*, Ankara: Anı Yayıncılık, 2006

- Kafesoğlu, İbrahim, *Türk Milli Kültürü*, İstanbul: Boğaziçi Yayınları, 1995.

- Köseoğlu, Nevzat, *Türk Dünyası Tarihi ve Türk Medeniyeti Üzerine Düşünceler*, İstanbul: Ötüken, 1997.

- Lewis, Bernard, *The Emergence of Modern Turkey*, Oxford: Oxford University Press, 2001.

- Lord Kinross, *Atatürk: Bir Milletin Yeniden Doğuşu*, İstanbul: Altın Kitaplar, 2006.

- Mango, Andrew, *Atatürk: The Biography of the Founder of Modern Turkey*, John Murray, 2004.

- Mango, Andrew, *The Turks Today*, Woodstock: The Overlook Press, 2004.

- Merçil, Erdoğan, *Müslüman Türk Devletleri Tarihi*, Ankara: TTK, 1991.

- Merçil, Erdoğan, *Büyük Selçuklu Devleti Siyasi Tarihi*, Ankara: Nobel Yayın, 2005.

- Oran Baskın, (ed.), *Türk Dış Politikası*, İstanbul: İletişim, 2001.

- Ortaylı, İlber, *Osmanlı İmparatorluğu'nda Alman Nüfuzu*, İstanbul: Alkım, 2006.

- Özey, Ramazan, *Türk Dünyası*, İstanbul: Eğitim, 1997.

-Rasonyi, Laszlo, *Tarihte Türklük*, Ankara: Türk Kültürünü Araştırma Enstitüsü, 1993.

- Roux, Jean-Paul, *Türklerin Tarihi: Pasifik'ten Akdeniz'e 2000 yılı*, İstanbul: Kabalcı, 2007.

- Sevim, A. & Yücel, Y., *Türkiye Tarihi: Fetih, Selçuklu ve Beylikler Dönemi*, Ankara: TTK, 1989.

- Sevim, A. & Merçil, E., *Selçuklu Devletleri Tarihi: Siyaset, Teşkilat ve Kültür*, Ankara: TTK, 1995.

- Seydi, Süleyman, *The Turkish Straits and the Great Powers: From the Montreaux Convention to the Early Cold War, 1936-1947*, İstanbul: the Isis Pres, 2003.

- Shaw, Stanford, *History of the Ottoman Empire and Modern Turkey, Vol I; Empire of Gazis: The Rise and Decline of the Ottoman Empire 1290–1808*, Cambridge: Cambridge University Press, 1976

- Sonyel, Salahi Ramsdan, *Turkish Diplomacy 1918-1923: Mustafa Kemal and the Turkish National Movement*, London: SAGE, 1975.

-Şahin, Muhammet, *Türk Tarihi ve Kültürü*, Ankara: Gündüz Eğitim ve Yayıncılık, 2003.

- Turan, Ahmet Nezihi (ed.), Tarih El Kitabı: *Selçuklulardan Bugüne*, Ankara: Grafiker, 2004.

- Turan, Osman, *Selçuklular Zamanında Türkiye*, İstanbul: Ötüken, 2004.

- *Türk Dünyası El Kitabı*, Birinci Cilt, Ankara: Türk Kültürünü Araştırma Enstitüsü, 1992.

- *The Important Events of Turkish History*, Ankara: The General Staff Printing House, 2003.

- Yazıcı, Nesimi, *İlk Türk - İslam Devletleri Tarihi*, Ankara: Türk Diyanet Vakfı, 2005.

- Yücel, Yaşar, *Timur'un Ortadoğu - Anadolu Seferleri ve Sonuçları (1393 - 1402)*, Ankara: TTK, 1989.

- Zürcher, Erik Jan, *Modernleşen Türkiye'nin Tarihi*, İstanbul: İletişim Yayınları, 2006.

- www.theottomans.org

- http://en.wikipedia.org

# ANNEX

## The Family Tree of Seljuk

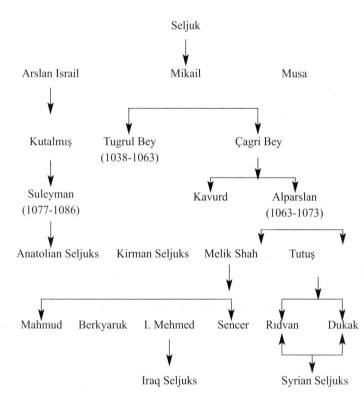

# The Lists of Anatolian Seljuk Sultans

| | |
|---|---|
| Suleyman I | 1077-1086 |
| Kılıçarslan I | 1092-1107 |
| Melik Shah1 | 1107-1116 |
| Mesud I | 1116-1155 |
| Kılıçarslan II | 1155-1192 |
| Keyhusrev I | 1192-1196 |
| Suleyman II | 1196-1204 |
| Kılıçarslan III | 1204 |
| Keyhusrev I (second time) | 1204-1210 |
| Keykavus I | 1210-1219 |
| Alaeddin Keykubad I | 1219-1237 |
| Keyhusrev II | 1237-1246 |
| Keykavus II | 1246-1260 |
| Kılıçarslan IV | 1248-1265 |
| Alaaddin Keykubad II | 1249-1257 |
| Keyhusrev II | 1265-1282 |
| Mesud II | 1281-1284 |
| Alaaddin Keykubad III | 1284 |
| Mesud II (Second time) | 1284-1293 |
| Alaaddin Keykubad III | 1293-1294 |
| Mesud II (Third time) | 1294-1301 |
| Alaaddin Keykubad III (third time) | 1301-1303 |
| Mesud II (fourth time) | 1303-1307 |

# The Lists of Ottoman Sultans

| | |
|---|---|
| Osman I | 1299-1326 |
| Orhan Ghazi | 1326-1359 |
| Murad I | 1359-1389 |
| Bayezid I | 1389-1402 |
| Mehmed I | 1413-1421 |
| Murad II | 1421-1451 |
| Mehmed II | 1451-1581 |
| Bayezid II | 1481-1512 |
| Selim I | 1512-1520 |
| Suleyman I | 1520-1566 |
| Selim II | 1566-1574 |

| | |
|---|---|
| Murad III | 1574-1595 |
| Mehmed III | 1595-1603 |
| Ahmed I | 1603-1622 |
| Mustafa I | 1622-1623 |
| Osman II | 1618-1622 |
| Murad VI | 1623-1640 |
| Ibrahim | 1640-1648 |
| Mehmed IV | 1648-1687 |
| Suleyman II | 1687-1691 |
| Ahmed II | 1691-1695 |
| Mustafa II | 1695-1703 |
| Ahmed III | 1703-1730 |
| Mahmud I | 1730-1754 |
| Osman III | 1754-1757 |
| Mustafa III | 1757-1774 |
| Abdulhamid I | 1774-1789 |
| Selim III | 1789-1807 |
| Mustafa IV | 1807-1808 |
| Mahmud II | 1808-1839 |
| Abdulmecid | 1839-1861 |
| Abdulaziz | 1861-1876 |
| Murad V | 1876 |
| Abdulhamid II | 1876-1909 |
| Mehmed V | 1909-1918 |
| Mehmed VI | 1918-1922 |

# The Presidents of Turkish Republic

| | |
|---|---|
| Mustafa Kemal Atatürk | 1923-1938 |
| İsmet İnönü | 1938-1950 |
| Celal Bayar | 1950-1960 |
| Cemal Gürsel | 1960-1966 |
| Cevdet Sunay | 1966-1973 |
| Fahri Korutürk | 1973-1980 |
| Kenan Evren | 1982-1989 |
| Turgut Özal | 1989-1993 |
| Süleyman Demirel | 1993-2000 |
| Ahmet Necdet Sezer | 2000-2007 |
| Abdullah Gül | 2007- |